Guided Mindfulness Meditations for Deep Sleep, Overcoming Anxiety & Stress Relief: Beginners Meditation Scripts For Relaxation, Insomnia & Chakras Healing, Awakening & Balance

By Meditation Made Effortless

Notes for the narrator:

-Triple spacing indicates longer pauses.
-Certain meditations may require a hypnosis-styled voice.

Table of Contents:

Total Body Rejuvenation | 60 Minutes | 2312 Words 1

Morning Gratitude | 15 Minutes | 1297 Words 15

Lower Anxiety Fast | 15 minutes | 1474 Words 26

Calm Down the Mind | 15 Minutes | 881 Words 36

Peaceful Nap | 30 Minutes |1324 Words 43

Prepare For Sleep | 30 Minutes | 1656 Words 53

Guided Sleep Meditation | 60 Minutes | 875 Words 68

Lunch Break Relaxation | 15 Minutes | 1221 Words 79

After Work Relaxation | 30 Minutes | 1885 Words 88

Calm Yourself After a Panic Attack | 30 Minutes | Words 1557 101

Quick Relaxation Through Visualization | 15 Minutes | 1184 Words 113

Affirmations for Deep Healing | 30 Minutes | 1115 Words 122

Deep Healing | 60 Minutes | 2632 Words 133

Recharge Your Energy | 30 Minutes | Words 2237 154

Clear Your Mind | 60 Minutes | 1670 words 170

Visualize Your Ideal Day | 15 Minutes | 942 Words ... 183

Manifesting Your Dreams | 60 Minutes | 2245 Words 190

Self-Love and Compassion | 30 Minutes | 1133 Words 205

Meet Your Inner Child | 60 Minutes | 2326 Words 213

Total Body Rejuvenation | 60 Minutes | 2312 Words

Hello and welcome to this sixty minute meditation for total body rejuvenation. We will be working with your different chakras to show you how to pull energy into them. For this meditation it may help to view your body like a battery. Yes, we need to fuel ourselves with excellent nutrition, maintain energy with exercise, and clear our minds for optimal performance, however we also need to understand that energy is something we can absorb into our bodies. It is very simple, and you should be able to feel the results after the meditation. You can listen to this meditation whenever you need to rejuvenate some part of your mind, body, or emotions.

To begin, make sure you are somewhere comfortable where you will not be disturbed for the next sixty minutes. You can either sit, or lie down, and if you fall asleep during this meditation that is perfectly okay. As energizing as it is to pull energy into the body, it can also be soothing at the same time. Always listen to what your body wants to do first.

As you get comfortable, check that your spine is straight- this will allow energy to flow down into your body in an easier way. Having excellent posture allows your nervous system to be in alignment and having a calm nervous system allows a lot more energy to flow within you.

Bring your conscious awareness to your breath.

See if you can play with your breath in your body. Pull it down to the bottom of your abdomen and breathe from here for a while.

Try breathing so that you are expanding the sides of your ribcage.

And try breathing into your chest, expanding all areas here.

Letting your breath move around your chest to your abdomen and find a point in your body where it feels best to breathe today. Each day your breathing may be a bit different. Some days you may prefer to breathe from the very bottom of your abdomen or your diaphragm. Some days it may be more comfortable to keep your breathing a little higher. See what feels best for you. Find your natural position of breathing today, without any judgement.

Wherever you have decided to breathe, allow your exhalations to be longer than your inhalations. Witness any effects this has on your body.

Perhaps add a pause between your inhalations and your exhalations if that feels natural to you to do so.

Find the rhythm breathing that feels the most natural and healthy for you. You will be maintaining this rhythm for the next sixty minutes, so you don't have to make it too different from your natural breathing tempo, just a bit slower, and a bit deeper.

There is a chakra located at the very top of your scalp. In english this is known as the crown chakra. This is where energy can enter your body. You can also think of it like a beautiful flower that absorbs the sun.

Imagine that there is a sun above you. It can be any color: purple, pink, gold, yellow, white, iridescent, or whatever feels best for you. The crown chakra at the top of your head begins to absorb the sun's energy. It is okay if it is nighttime when you are listening to this, or if you are indoors, you are just going to imagine that a sun is shining down into your crown chakra.

Your crown chakra, as you breathe, will absorb this energy into your body. It may be a little trickle at first, but as you get the hang of it and ease into it, it may flow heavier and more assuredly with time.

Breathing into this sensation- the crown chakra absorbing a sun's energy like a flower.

Feeling this light being absorbed into your body. Into every cell, every bone, every muscle, every organ.

If it helps, you can move your breathing to the back of your neck. You may make a sound as you breathe in and out. It feels like pulling the current of air into the back of your throat as you breathe in and out, still keeping the tempo and depth of your breath the same.

Moving down to what is known as the third eye chakra. This is in the center of your forehead, in between your eyebrows, and also a few inches back into your brain. It is also where the pineal gland is located, which is seen as a very sacred and powerful part of the mind. This is where your imagination and divination lives.

Allow the sun's beautiful energy to flow into the crown chakra and then wrap around the third eye chakra. Feeling the light pool into this area, stimulating it gently. Breathing into here if it helps.

Letting whatever happens, happen here. Feeling the light pooling into third eye chakra as you breathe deeply with your body.

Letting go of anything that you no longer need, and just enjoying the sensation of the sun warming up your third eye chakra.

Moving down into the throat chakra. This is located in the middle of your throat. Letting the light from above shine down your crown chakra, to your third eye chakra, all the way down to your beautiful throat. This is the home of your voice, your thyroid, and so many delicate parts of your body. This sacred space is where you share your personal ideas with the external world. Letting this light gently wrap around this area and provide it with warmth and healing energy.

Breathing into your throat chakra if it helps to absorb the light.

Letting go of any expectations of what might happen here.

Continue your deep breathing.

Letting the sun shine down your body even more, as it spreads to your arms and your hands and down to your heart chakra. This is located in the middle of your chest, around where your heart is. If you wish you can put a hand over your heart chakra to connect with it more.

The light from above shines down your crown chakra, down to your third eye chakra, down to your throat chakra, through your arms, and then to your heart chakra. This is where you feel the connection with energy around you. This is where you have compassion and love for yourself and others. Breathing into here if it helps, as you let the light wrap around this area. Providing your heart with light and love and warmth. Feeling the sun's rays shine down upon your heart chakra. Letting it fill you with its love.

Keeping your breathing deep and steady.

The light from above shines down your body and moves to your solar plexus chakra. This is located a few inches above your belly button. It is a large source of power, confidence and self worth. If it helps, you can put your hand over here as you breathe into this area. The light from above shines into your crown chakra, into your third eye chakra, into your throat chakra, down into your arms and then to your heart chakra, lowering into your solar plexus chakra.

Breathing into here as the light wraps around this area.

Fueling your abdomen with power, light, tranquility and peace.

This sunlight from above shines down your crown chakra, to your third eye chakra, to your throat chakra, down to your arms back to your heart chakra, down to your solar plexus chakra, and then flowing into your sacral chakra. The sacral chakra is the home to your creativity and pleasure. This chakra is located just below your belly button in the center of your body. Feel free to put your hand over this area as you breathe into it if it helps to connect.

The light wraps around this area and gently stimulates it with its love and warmth. This area is full of creative, sexual, and intuitive power. Breathing into here as you let the light from above enter and heal all parts of this area.

Breathing gently as you do this.

Letting go anything that comes up.

Moving a little lower into your root chakra, this is located at the base of your spine. Breathing into here as you feel the light pouring in from your crown chakra, down into your third eye chakra, down into your throat chakra, down into your arms and then your heart chakra, down into your solar plexus chakra, down into your sacral chakra, and finally into your root chakra. In this chakra you can put your hand at the base of your torso or breathe into here if it helps to connect. This chakra is in charge of a feeling of safe, secure, and protected. It is our direct connection to the Earth- hence "root" chakra.

Breathing gently and slowly. Allowing light to flow into this area and fill this chakra with support, energy, and love.

Letting the light flow down your legs into Earth.

Being in the flow of the light shining from the top of your head, down your body and arms, down your legs, and into the Earth.

Feeling the flow of energy from this sunlight above, through your body, into the Earth.

Breathing in, accepting any light in any area of your body that needs it.

Letting anything go that you no longer need.

Feeling the sensation of gravity holding your body down and hugging you closer to Earth.

Imagine that, as the top of your head is like a flower absorbing the light from above, your legs are like the roots into the Earth. These roots grow further and further into the Earth's core. Moving deeper into the Earth's crust, past all the layers, and into the center of the Earth.

In this center of the Earth there is a powerful center that you can tap into. It can be seen like the Earth's internal sun, or like a massive source of energy to pull from.

As light shines down upon you from above, Earth shines up towards you from below. Earth provides a grounding, soothing energy that balances out what the light above gives you.

Breathing in this energy from the Earth. Feeling its grounding presence surging up your legs into your root chakra. Feeling the Earth fuel this area with stability, love, light, and power.

Breathing into this area, and putting your hand over your root chakra if you feel inspired to.

Letting yourself be in the flow from the light above pouring into your body into the Earth, and the Earth sending energy back up up into your body.

The energy from the Earth moves up your roots, into the root chakra, and up to the sacral chakra, pooling into here. Your sacral chakra absorbs it in the best way for you. Breathing in this energy. Letting it integrate into your body.

Breathing in this grounding energy as it moves up the sacral chakra into the solar plexus chakra.

Letting anything go that you do not need, and receiving the beautiful energy from the Earth into your solar plexus area. Breathing into here.

Letting the energy move up into your heart chakra. Breathing into here as the Earth provides you with warm, soothing, and grounding energy.

Letting this energy move up your arms, and then all the way back up into your throat chakra. Breathing into here as the Earth provides you with grounding, soothing energy into this area.

Letting everything go that comes up. It may not be yours to hold on to. Just receive this grounding energy.

Letting the energy move up into your third eye. Grounding this area. Providing it with energetic nutrients, love, and compassion. Breathing into here.

Letting it move up all the way into your crown chakra- the flower part. Letting the Earth energy soothe this area, ground it, and provide it with love and compassion.

Letting the energy flow past your crown chakra, up into the sun above you. Letting the Earth's energy merge with the sun above.

The sunlight from above flows down your body, into the Earth, and that energy flows back up your body, into the light above you.

Being in the current of both energies like a battery. The energy above being light, rich, and rejuvenating. The Energy below being grounding, healing, and nourishing.

Breathing into your whole body as you are connected to both energies.

Releasing any energy you no longer need to hold on to. Releasing any resistance. Releasing any fear. Releasing any stress. Releasing any shame. Releasing any guilt. Releasing what is not yours.

Embracing light. Embracing love. Embracing joy. Embracing peace. Embracing prosperity.

Embracing energy. Embracing rejuvenation. Embracing vitality. Embracing health. Embracing wealth. Embracing your true authenticity.

Staying here for as long as you need.

When you are ready, coming back into the sensations of your body.

Feel the temperature of your body.

Feel any heaviness or lightness anywhere.

Feel the sensation of clothing or fabric on your skin.

Feel the sensation of gravity holding you to Earth.

Hear any sounds surrounding you.

Smell any scents surrounding you.

Taste any flavors on your tongue.

Feel the sensation of your mouth.

Open your eyes when you are ready and take in the colors. Take in the shapes. Take in the light versus shadow.

Become present in your current surroundings once more.

Take as long as you need before you go back to your usual day. Make sure you drink plenty of water today. Listen to this meditation any time you feel you need extra rejuvenation. Thank you for listening, and have a wonderful day.

Morning Gratitude | 15 Minutes | 1297 Words

Good morning and welcome to this fifteen minute guided meditation for increasing your gratitude! How we perceive the world dictates how the world perceives us. Someone who walks through life looking at what will go wrong will end up focusing on that, and will have a higher chance of it happening to them. Someone who focuses on what is going right sees more opportunities available to them, more friends around them, a safer world, and therefore has more of that optimistic energy available to them. It is like a snowball effect where daily practice of thankfulness will allow it to be your natural state. Looking at what is going right in your life will show you that you already have everything you need right here, right now. That you are complete, just as you are. That you are enough. That you are a beautiful person. Sometimes you just have to remember though. Let's begin.

Take a moment to get comfortable. It is recommended to experience this meditation sitting up with your spine straight. You can sit on the floor or in a chair. You may want to turn your electronics on to do not disturb so that the alerts do not distract you.

Connect with your breath.

Enjoy the sensation of air entering your body, and air leaving your body.

Keeping your breath at a gentle and steady pace.

Bringing all of your awareness to the sensation of breathing.

Feeling the rise of your abdomen as you inhale, and the fall of it as you exhale.

Breathing in refreshing morning air.

Breathing out any remaining fatigue.

Breathing in invigorating air.

Breathing out any stress.

Breathing in loving air.

Breathing out any tension in your body.

Letting your body relax with each breath.

Imagining that oxygen is nourishing every part of your body.

Feeling your breath nourishing your head.

Feeling your breath nourishing your neck.

Feeling your breath nourishing your chest and your upper back.

Feeling your breath nourishing your shoulders and upper arms.

Feeling your breath nourishing your elbows, your lower arms, and your hands.

Feeling your breath nourishing the middle of your torso.

Feeling your breath nourishing your belly, waist, and lower back.

Feeling your breath nourishing your hips, groin and buttocks.

Feeling your breath nourishing your upper legs and knees.

Feeling your breath nourishing your lower legs, ankles and feet.

Feeling your breath move through your entire body.

Each breath enters through your nose, to your lungs and spreads out to your whole body.

Each breath leaves your body, from your lungs, through your nose.

Letting the pacing of your breathing be as slow as you wish.

Imagine that the air you are breathing in is this beautiful light energy. It perhaps appears as a certain color to you. Maybe a pastel pink, purple, green, or a soothing blue. Whatever feels best for you. As you breathe in, this beautiful colored energy enters your body, soothing your cells.

Breathing in this energy. Its beautiful color entering through your nose into your body.

This beautiful energy mixing with your blood and bringing this energy to all parts of your body.

Exhaling out anything you wish to release.

Breathing in this energy.

Exhaling out anything you wish to release.

Breathing in this energy.

Exhaling out anything you wish to release.

Keep going for a little while.

Bring awareness to how amazing it is that you can breathe!

Noting how wonderful it is that you can breathe through your nose or mouth.

How breathtaking it is that this air moves down your throat and into your lungs.

How astonishing it is that your lungs move oxygen from the air into your blood.

How magical it is that this blood is then pumped from your heart to the rest of your body.

How wondrous it is that all this happens without your conscious attention to it. That your body is so intelligent, it can take care of itself without your conscious awareness of what is even going on!

What other parts of your body are doing magical things without your conscious awareness?

What other parts of life are just as magical?

Taking a moment, as you continue to breathe, to just notice what is magical about your life.

Breathing through your abdomen as you do this.

Exhaling out any tension.

What other parts of your life are you grateful for?

What people in your life are you grateful for?

What memories in your life are you grateful for?

What about yourself are you grateful for?

What about today are you grateful for?

What about this very moment, as you listen to this meditation, are you grateful for?

What about your body are you grateful for?

What about your work, your passions, or your job are you grateful for?

What are you grateful for about where you live?

What are you grateful for about your city of residence?

What are you grateful for about the country that you currently live in?

What are you grateful for about the room or location you are in?

What about life are you grateful for?

Taking some time to come into awareness of your feet. Perhaps noting one thing you are grateful for about your feet.

Feeling the sensations of your ankles. Noting one thing you are grateful for about your ankles.

Feeling the sensations of your lower legs. Noting one thing you are grateful for about your lower legs.

Feeling the sensations of your knees. Noting one thing you are grateful for about your knees.

Feeling the sensations of your upper legs. Noting one thing you are grateful for about your upper legs.

Feeling the sensations of your groin and buttocks. Noting one thing you are grateful for about your groin and buttocks.

Feeling the sensations of your hips. Noting one thing you are grateful for about your hips.

Feeling the sensations of your lower abdomen and lower back. Noting one thing you are grateful for about your lower abdomen and lower back.

Feeling the sensations of your waist area. Noting one thing you are grateful for about your waist area.

Feeling the sensations of your lower chest and surrounding back area. Noting one thing you are grateful for about your lower chest and surrounding back area.

Feeling the sensations of your chest and upper back. Noting one thing you are grateful for about your chest and upper back.

Feeling the sensations of your shoulders. Noting one thing you are grateful for about your shoulders.

Feeling the sensations of your upper arms. Noting one thing you are grateful for about your upper arms.

Feeling the sensations of your elbows. Noting one thing you are grateful for about your elbows.

Feeling the sensations of your lower arms. Noting one thing you are grateful for about your lower arms.

Feeling the sensations of your wrists and hands. Noting one thing you are grateful for about your wrists and hands.

Feeling the sensations of your neck. Noting one thing you are grateful for about your neck.

Feeling the sensations of your face. Noting one thing you are grateful for about your face.

Feeling the sensations of your head and skull. Noting one thing you are grateful for about your head and skull.

Opening your eyes when you are ready and just taking in the room around you.

Maybe taking a deep stretch when you're ready.

Taking some time to come back into your surroundings. Going as slowly as needed.

Thank you for listening to this meditation for gratitude. As you go through the rest of your day, take a moment to note what you are grateful for. Focusing on what you already have can help nurture a sense of fulfillment and joy within. You may notice that you have a lovely day without even trying.

Lower Anxiety Fast | 15 minutes | 1474 Words

Hello, and welcome to this meditation for lowering anxiety fast. You can listen to this at any point of the day. Please make sure you are not driving, operating machinery, or doing anything that requires your full attention. It is important to bring your total awareness to this meditation for the next fifteen minutes.

Take a moment to turn your electronics on to do not disturb. Make sure that wherever you are, you feel safe, comfortable, and relaxed. You can either sit or lie down, but make sure you feel like you can remain there for the next fifteen minutes in comfort.

Bring your awareness to your breath without changing anything about it, just noticing where it is.

Does it feel shallow? Does it feel deep?

Does your breath feel like it's in your upper chest area? Does it feel like it's in the middle of your chest? Does it feel like it's in your abdomen area? Does it feel like it's in your lower abdomen area?

Being present with the sensations of your breath in your body.

If possible, see if you can consciously lower your breathing into your abdomen or your lower abdomen. This will feel like you are breathing through your belly like how a baby breathes.

It may feel a bit foreign at first and that is perfectly okay. If it is too uncomfortable, just resume your normal breathing.

Taking slightly longer breaths in and out.

Letting your breathing enter a relaxing tempo.

If you feel comfortable doing this, allow your exhalations to be longer than your inhalations.

Taking the time to let your body relax, as you continue breathing into your belly.

You may notice that your mind begins to slow down as your body relaxes, or you may notice that your mind begins to speed up as your body relaxes, or perhaps it stays the same. Any experience is fine. We're bringing attention and awareness to what is happening right now without any judgement.

Notice if any sensations in your body are coming up to your awareness. Just noticing it without changing anything.

You may notice parts of your body relaxing. Just noticing it without changing anything.

Keeping your breathing going at a slow and comfortable pace for you.

Allowing your body to change naturally without any effort on your part.

We're going to do a body scan. This is a simple way to allow your body to relax. If your eyes are open, I recommend closing them now. If you get uncomfortable with your eyes closed at any point during this meditation, feel free to open them again. It simply allows for a deeper focus on your physical body.

Keep your breathing going at that wonderful slow pace. Imagine that all the tension, heaviness, and unnecessary energy from the very top of your head melts, and falls off of your body.

Just feel the visceral sensations, using your imagination, of any unnecessary energy leaving the top of your head, sliding down your body, and into the Earth beneath you.

Making sure that during this, your breathing stays at that wonderful slow pace.

Repeating this sensation to your eyebrow area, and around the head as well. Letting all tension from the forehead, to the eyebrows, and all around your scalp, just melt off your body, into the earth beneath you.

Letting each long exhalation take all this energy with it and releasing it.

Moving down to your eye area and around the scalp, letting all of this tension go. Using your exhalations to release it. Letting the energy slide down your body, and into the Earth beneath you.

Moving down to your cheek area, your ears, and the scalp behind them. Breathing in and letting everything go with your exhalations.

Now to your lips, your lower cheeks, your jaw, and the very top part of your neck. Breathing into here. On the exhalations, letting all of this tension go and let it slide down your body, into the Earth beneath you.

Allowing yourself to enjoy the sensations of relaxation arising within your body.

Now onto your neck. Breathing into here and letting all tension go with your exhalations.

Now to the very top part of your shoulders, including your collar bone. Breathing into here and letting it all go. Letting all the tension, stress, anxiety, and heavy emotions go.

Now making your way to your arms, focusing on your shoulders and upper arm area. Breathing into here, and on the exhalations, letting all tension and anxiety just drop away from your body into the Earth beneath you.

Now your elbows, your lower arms, and your hands. Breathing into here, and letting everything melt away, down into the Earth.

Now back up to the top part of your chest, just beneath your collar bone, wrapping around to the armpit area, and circling around to the strong back muscles. Breathing into here, and letting all tension, pain, or worries go on your exhalations. Imagining all the stress melting away into the Earth.

Lowering down to the pecks or breast area and all the muscles here, wrapping around the middle of the ribcage, and to the upper middle back. Breathing in, and letting all stress, heaviness, and dense energy go on the exhalations into the Earth beneath you.

Moving down to the lower rib cage area. Breathing into it. Allowing your awareness to wrap around the sides of the lower rib cage, and around the back. Just feeling any tension melting down from your body into the Earth.

Bringing your awareness to your abdomen area. This includes your abdomen, your waist, and just beneath the middle of your back. Breathing into here, and letting all the stress, anxiety, and tension go on your exhalations.

Now your lower abdomen, breathing into here, letting everything go in your lower abdomen, your hips, and your lower back. Releasing all tension, worry or anxiety down into the Earth beneath you.

Now to your groin area and your buttocks. Breathing into here, and letting all tension, heavy sensations, and unnecessary energy go on the exhalations into the Earth beneath you.

Focusing on your upper legs, keeping your breathing going here, allowing all the tension and stress to leave on the exhalations. Allowing the heavy energy to melt down into the Earth beneath you.

Now bring your awareness to your knees and your lower legs. Breathing into here and letting all the tension, stress, and anxiety go into the Earth beneath you. Feeling it just melt away from your body.

Bringing your awareness to your ankles and your feet. Breathing into here, and letting all the micro tension, stress, and anxiety melt into the Earth on your exhalation.

Now taking a moment to breathe. Enjoying how your body feels.

Bringing your awareness to the entirety of your body, take a deep breath in, and let everything out on a deep, luxurious exhalation.

Breathing into your body, and letting everything go again.

Feel as though you could breathe into your entire body and have all remaining stress, tension and anxiety melting away into the Earth beneath you.

When you are ready, taking some time to notice how your body feels now. Are there any differences you can feel?

Gently bring your awareness to observe what you are hearing. Noticing any environmental sounds. Noticing the sound of this recording. Noticing the sound of your breathing. Bringing your awareness to any sounds around you.

Bringing your awareness to your sense of smell. Breathing in and noticing the light scents in the air.

Bringing your awareness to your sense of taste. How does your tongue feel? What are you tasting right now? Are you thirsty or quenched?

Bringing your awareness to your sense of touch. Noticing the fabric gently touching your body. Noticing the sensation of gravity. Noticing the sensation of your body resting on a chair, on the ground.

And whenever you are ready, opening your eyes slowly, and taking in the surrounding environment. Noticing the surrounding colours. Noticing the surrounding shapes. Noticing the surrounding light and shadows.

Take one final deep breath in and out. Letting everything go.

Thanking yourself and your body for participating in this meditation.

Thank you for listening to this meditation. For the rest of the day be gentle to yourself. A lot of anxiety can be caused by how we treat ourselves. Releasing patterns of anxious thinking, actions, and behavior can take time. By practicing meditation or anything that can pull you into a healthy state of being, it will eventually become natural for you to feel less anxious. Notice the difference between how you feel today versus how you feel on days where you don't meditate or consciously relax. It may be tiny changes, but over time these positive effects will compound into noticeable daily results.

Have a relaxing rest of your day.

Calm Down the Mind | 15 Minutes | 881 Words

Hello and welcome to this meditation for calming down the mind in fifteen minutes. Please make sure you are in a comfortable position and that you will not be disturbed for the duration of this meditation.

Take a moment to relax.

Let your day go, your responsibilities go, your to-do list go, and your worries go.

During this meditation you are just here, in this present moment.

You are just your breath. You are just experiencing this. You are just here, and now.

Simplicity is powerful.

Let your exhalations be longer than your inhalations. Allowing your breath to slow down to a tempo that is comfortable but relaxing.

Watching the mind is something that can be very revealing about our individual thought patterns. Many times there are more thoughts going on in the mind than we realize, and the thoughts can be repetitive and not necessarily beneficial. Thoughts can dart around, circle back, or jump from concept to concept in a nonsensical fashion. Sometimes it is like a little child that is allowed to roam free in a house so they can do anything they want- they jump and run around everywhere, and move from one object to another all day long. In bringing awareness to how our thoughts are, we can begin to slow the thoughts down, and be aware of our relationship to them. With a relationship with our thoughts they can begin to work with us in a slower and more logical fashion. It is like turning an unused tool into something that can work with us instead of against us. We can learn to love our thoughts, and in turn our thoughts will work with us.

For a moment, see if you can make your mind go blank. It is okay if thoughts pop up, but let your mind just relax.

Let all of your thoughts go. A lot of energy can be used up by the mind, so the first step in identifying what the mind is doing is by bringing awareness to it.

See if you can listen or watch the thoughts in your mind without judgement.

For every thought that comes up, note it with a "thank you thought", then release the thought with "and I release you."

So, "Thank you thought, and I release you." to every thought that comes into your awareness. Keep your breathing slow and gentle as you do this.

A thought comes in "Thank you thought, and I release you."

Another thought comes in, "Thank you thought, and I release you."

Letting your mind slow down, and accepting any thought that comes up. All thoughts are welcome.

Sometimes the thought may not be a clear thought, it may not make any sense, it is still: "Thank you thought, and I release you."

Some of you may notice a silence beginning to form between thoughts, you can also pay attention to the silence. When a thought pops up, simply saying: "Thank you thought, and I release you." and returning to the silence until the next thought comes in.

Letting the appreciated thoughts drift away. They may come back and that's okay. "Thank you thought, and I release you."

Allowing your breath to be gentle and slow.

Breathing in and out as you let your thoughts go.

You are not your mind, or your thoughts.

You experience having a mind, and you experience having thoughts, but they are not you fundamentally.

Noticing the silence forming between the thoughts.

Noticing the space forming between the thoughts.

Noticing the emptiness forming between the thoughts.

Allowing the thoughts, but letting them go: "Thank you thought, and I release you."

Breathing as you are experiencing this.

Letting all of your thoughts go with appreciation and kindness towards them. Thoughts are not our enemy, they are here to help us, we just need to build a relationship to them.

Letting the mind slow down.

Letting any stress, anxiety, or worry go.

Feeling it melt away from your mind.

Letting your mind go blank, and when the occasional thought comes up "Thank you thought, and I release you."

Being present with your breath.

Bringing your mind's eye away from your thoughts, and onto your breathing.

Feeling the sensations as you breathe in, and out.

In, and out.

In, and out.

In, and out.

Coming back into the sensations of your body.

Bringing awareness to the sounds around you.

The scents around you.

The sensations of your body.

The taste on your tongue.

And opening your eyes, noticing the light and shadows. Noticing the textures around you. Noting the colour.

Thank you for listening to this meditation. Throughout the day you can release your thoughts with this "Thank you thought, and I release you." sentence. It is okay if you have a day full of thoughts, it is a habit. Eventually, with practice, you can get to a point where you are familiar with the feeling of the silence between the thoughts. The thoughts may always be there, but it gets easier to come back to the neutral silent state every time you do it. Practice is key here. Finding ways to enjoy the act of watching the thoughts. As time passes you may notice some interesting positive side effects from doing this.

Have a lovely day. Goodbye.

Peaceful Nap | 30 Minutes |1324 Words

Hello and welcome to this guided meditation for a peaceful nap. This lasts for thirty minutes. Make sure to turn your electronics on to do not disturb and to set your alarm for when you need to wake up if needed.

Wherever you are, get comfortable. Pull your blanket over you, fluff your pillow, and relax your body.

For the next thirty minutes you can let go of every single part of your life. You can let go of your work, your responsibilities, your duties, your errands, or anything else that is hovering over your shoulder. You can let go of your relationships, of your thoughts, of your opinions, and just be present in this wonderful moment of relaxation.

It is okay if you don't fall asleep during this meditation. The act of closing your eyes and resting is enough to allow your body, mind, and emotions to have a break.

Being present with your breath.

Being present with how your body feels.

Being present with what may be coming up in your mind.

Letting it all just flow in and out of your awareness. Not holding onto anything, but simply letting things come into your awareness, and flowing away from your awareness like water in a stream.

Slowing down your breath. Imagining that your body is already in deep sleep.

Everything in your body is slowing down. Your heartbeat, your thoughts, your movement, your sensations.

Breathing in, and out.

In, and out.

In, and out.

Slowing everything down.

Letting your mind go. Letting your intellect go.

On your exhalations, letting any stress or anxiety go.

Breathing in peaceful energy.

Breathing out stress.

Allowing your breath to fill up your entire body, and exhale with the sensation of breathing out of your entire body.

Breathing in soothing energy that fills every cell in your body.

Breathing out any anxiety, tension, or stress that you no longer need.

Breathing in relaxing and tranquil energy.

Breathing out any uncomfortable energy you no longer need.

Breathing in soothing energy.

Breathing out into relaxation.

Breathing in soothing energy.

Breathing out into relaxation.

Breathing in soothing energy.

Breathing out into relaxation.

Keep your breathing going at a comfortable and relaxing tempo. See if you can breathe from the bottom of your diaphragm, which is in your abdomen.

Perhaps allowing the air to flow in and out of your body from the back of your throat, and this may produce a small sound as you breathe. Pulling air into the back of your throat and breathing out from the back of your throat.

Letting everything go even more.

Letting your thoughts go.

Letting your worries go.

Letting any stress go.

Focusing on your breathing, and nothing else.

Feeling any heaviness from your body melt away into the Earth.

Feeling any anxiety, tension or stress from your head and face melting into the Earth. It falls through your pillow, into the Earth, and away from your body forever.

Breathing as you are experiencing this.

Feeling any heaviness, tension, or stress from your neck melting into your pillow, into the Earth beneath you.

Feeling any pain, heaviness, or stress from the top of your torso and your shoulders melting away into the Earth beneath you. Falling through the mattress or surface you are laying on, and into the Earth.

Feeling any tension, anxiety, or stress melting away from your upper arms into the earth beneath you. Enjoying the sensations as you witness it melting away from your body forever.

Feeling any heaviness melt away from your elbows and lower arms. Breathing in, and releasing everything on your exhalations. Witnessing as this energy falls into the Earth and away from your body forever.

Moving your awareness to your wrists and hands, noting any stress, tension, or anxiety here and having it flow out of your wrists and hands into the Earth beneath you.

Keeping your breathing slow and steady from your abdomen as you experience this relaxation.

Moving up to your torso again, into your upper chest and upper back area. Breathing into here as all the stress, tension, or anxiety melts away into the Earth beneath you.

Breathing into the middle of your torso and back as you release all the tension, stress, or anxiety here. Letting everything go as it falls through the surface you are laying on, into the Earth and away from your body forever. This is not yours to hold on to anymore. Perhaps it never was.

Moving to your lower torso and back, feeling all the pressure, stress, and anxiety just melting away into the Earth beneath you. Witnessing as it falls through the surface you are laying on into the Earth forever.

Moving to your hips, groin, and buttocks area. Breathing into here, and letting everything go on your exhalation. Witnessing as it flows out of your body and into the Earth beneath you, where it is no longer yours to hold on to.

Moving to the upper legs, letting everything go on the exhalation into the Earth beneath you.

Moving to your knees and lower legs. Breathing into here, letting everything go on the exhalation. Witnessing as it flows into the Earth and away from your body.

Moving to your ankles and feet, breathing into here, letting all tension, stress, and anxiety go on your exhalations. It flows into the Earth and away from your body forever.

Feeling your whole body in such a relaxed state. Breathing in, and letting any remaining stress, tension, worry, pain or anxiety just melt away from you into the Earth forever. It is no longer yours to hold on to.

Breathing in, and letting everything go on the exhalations.

Breathing in, and letting everything go on the exhalations.

Breathing in, and letting everything go on the exhalations.

Taking some time to note how wonderful and relaxed your body feels right now.

Using your imagination, let's bring this relaxation to a deeper level. You are floating in a stream and this beautiful crystal clear water is flowing around you.

This nurturing water takes away any pain, tension, stress, heaviness, or unpleasant emotions and replaces it with soothing and loving energy.

As you breathe in, you feel crisp clean air entering your body, and as you breathe out you feel your body entering a deeper state of relaxation. Your head is comfortably above the water, and your body gently floats on the surface. It's a shallow amount of water, so if you ever want to stand up you can easily do so. The water flows around you gently and takes away any unwanted sensations.

As you breathe in, embrace this cool comforting air. As you breathe out, allow the water to take anything it wishes to take with it.

It may be old energies you no longer need, or anything in your body you no longer wish to hold on to.

Breathing in soothing energy from this experience, and breathing out anything you no longer wish to hold on to, allowing the water to gently carry it away forever.

Enjoy sitting in the stream, having your thoughts, emotions, and old energies float away from you, peacefully down the stream, away from your body.

Anything that is heavy or unpleasant is no longer yours to hold on to, simply releasing it to the water.

Feeling the water flow over all parts of your body. Notice the perfect temperature and soothing sensations.

Letting it flow around you, and taking away anything you no longer need.

Perhaps feeling the warm sun on your skin from above, as you breathe in the cool air.

Just enjoying this for a while.

As we bring this meditation to a close, you can either stay in this imagery, or come out of it, whatever feels best for you.

Just noticing how comfortable you are, wherever you are.

Noticing how safe you feel.

Noticing how relaxed you are.

Thank you for listening, have a lovely rest of your nap.

Prepare For Sleep | 30 Minutes | 1656 Words

Hello and welcome to this meditation for preparing for sleep. If you reach the end of this meditation and you are still awake, that is perfectly okay. The act of slowing down your mind, relaxing your body, and breathing deeply is very rejuvenating for your body. If possible, it is recommended to not move during the next thirty minutes of this guided meditation. That will bring a deeper layer of relaxation to the body as it gives it time to relax. You may want to take a moment to set your alarm, close your door, or whatever you need to do to prepare for sleep. Please pause this now if needed.

Either keep your eyes open or closed but settle down your body for the night. Taking a moment to relax everything and letting go of your day.

Letting go of what you have to do tomorrow, knowing you will get to it when you get to it.

Letting go of any responsibilities. You are here now, simply listening to this recording, and being present with your body, that is all.

Let's calm down the nervous system. This can help your body feel deeply relaxed from the inside out.

This breathing exercise is about breathing into your diaphragm. You will breathe in for four seconds, you will then hold your breath for four seconds, you will then breath out slowly for six seconds, and then hold again for two seconds. I will guide you through this. If you feel comfortable to add this, perform all of your breathing through the back of your throat. It may make a noise as you breathe, which is natural. It's like pulling the channel of air into the back of the throat rather than the through center of the throat.

Breathe in for four seconds.

Hold for four seconds.

Breathe out for six seconds.

Hold for two seconds.

Breathe in for four seconds.

Hold for four seconds.

Breathe out for six seconds.

Hold for two seconds.

Breathe in for four seconds.

Hold for four seconds.

Breathe out for six seconds.

Hold for two seconds.

Breathe in for four seconds.

Hold for four seconds.

Breathe out for six seconds.

Hold for two seconds.

Breathe in for four seconds.

Hold for four seconds.

Breathe out for six seconds.

Hold for two seconds.

Breathe in for four seconds.

Hold for four seconds.

Breathe out for six seconds.

Hold for two seconds.

Breathe in for four seconds.

Hold for four seconds.

Breathe out for six seconds.

Hold for two seconds.

Breathe in for four seconds.

Hold for four seconds.

Breathe out for six seconds.

Hold for two seconds.

Breathe in for four seconds.

Hold for four seconds.

Breathe out for six seconds.

Hold for two seconds.

Breathe in for four seconds.

Hold for four seconds.

Breathe out for six seconds.

Hold for two seconds.

Breathe in for four seconds.

Hold for four seconds.

Breathe out for six seconds.

Hold for two seconds.

Breathe in for four seconds.

Hold for four seconds.

Breathe out for six seconds.

Hold for two seconds.

Breathe in for four seconds.

Hold for four seconds.

Breathe out for six seconds.

Hold for two seconds.

Breathe in for four seconds.

Hold for four seconds.

Breathe out for six seconds.

Hold for two seconds.

Breathe in for four seconds.

Hold for four seconds.

Breathe out for six seconds.

Hold for two seconds.

Breathe in for four seconds.

Hold for four seconds.

Breathe out for six seconds.

Hold for two seconds.

Continue this tempo to the best of your ability as I guide you through deeper relaxation. If your breathing tempo changes, that is perfectly okay, let it evolve into what feels best for you.

Imagine that all your emotions in your body could relax. You feel serene, content, and peaceful. An easy way to achieve this state is to consider what you are grateful about. Gratitude causes our perception to focus on what is working in our favor, and is a simple mood booster.

Consider, while you are breathing, what went well for you today? What are you grateful for about your day today? It could be something small, or something big. Whatever you wish.

How did it make you feel, this thing that you are grateful for?

What are you grateful for about your physical body? It can be something you overlook, like how wonderful it is to breathe, or something you want to give your attention to, like how beautiful you are. Whatever feels best for you.

How does it make you feel, to feel this gratitude about your body?

Keeping your breathing going, at a pace that feels best for you, but that is relaxing.

What about sleep are you grateful for? It could be anything at all, have fun with this! Perhaps dreaming, perhaps how relaxing it is, perhaps how you can just let go of everything for a little while.

How does it make you feel, to feel this gratitude towards sleep?

What are you grateful for about who you are? What about you makes you feel gratitude about you? Have fun with this, let whatever comes up come up, no matter how small or large.

Breathing through this, deeply and slowly. Comfortably and relaxing.

Noting how it makes you feel to be grateful for yourself.

Focusing on your physical sensations now, let's just slowly relax your physical body. Letting go of the gratitude questions, but keeping the feeling alive within you. Keeping your breathing at this slow and steady pace.

Starting with your forehead, relaxing all the muscles here. Breathing into here, and relaxing all parts of your forehead. Taking your time, enjoying this.

Now moving to your scalp all around your head, really relaxing every tiny muscle. Taking your time.

Continuing with your deep breathing, moving to your eyes, relaxing here. Letting all the tension or tiny contractions go.

Moving to your cheeks, relaxing all areas here.

Relaxing all parts of your ears, all around it.

Relaxing your jaw, all the muscles that can be tense without you realizing it.

Relaxing your mouth, all the little muscles around the area.

Relaxing your tongue, and all muscles in your mouth.

Breathing as you do this, gently and slowly.

Moving your awareness down to your neck, gently relaxing all areas here. Breathing into here perhaps as you let all the tiny muscles go. Letting all the tension go.

Breathing and relaxing into your upper chest area including your clavicle bone area and the very top of your shoulders. Letting all the tension and stress go.

Sliding down into your shoulders, relaxing all areas here, even your underarm area. Breathing into here if that helps. Relaxing everything you feel is tense.

Moving down to your upper arms. Relaxing all the muscles here, all the tension.

Keeping your breath going.

Moving to your elbows and lower arms. Breathing and just letting all the tension go. Letting all the tiny amounts of stress and tension go.

Continuing down to your wrists and hands, breathing into all areas of it, and letting all the tiny muscles go. Perhaps noticing one finger relax at a time.

Moving back up to your shoulder blades and upper back. Breathing into here and letting all the tension go.

Moving around to your chest, relaxing all the muscles here, letting your breath relax the area.

Breathing into the middle of your back and relaxing all areas here.

Moving back around to your upper abdomen and relaxing the muscles and tension here. Letting everything go that is tense or stressed.

Wrapping around to your lower back and releasing all the tension, stress, and unpleasant sensations.

Moving around to your lower abdomen and waist, letting everything go with your breath. Breathing into here gently and slowly.

Moving around to your buttocks area, just relaxing everything.

Your hips, letting all the tiny muscles and tense sensations go.

Your groin area and pelvic floor, letting this area go. Breathing into here. Taking your time.

Relaxing your upper legs, letting go of all the stress and tension here. Letting it go until you feel a sense of relaxation emerging.

Moving to your knees and lower legs, releasing all the tiny tension and muscles being held here. Breathing into this area. Letting everything go.

Finally, your ankles and your feet, letting all the tension, stress, and muscles go.

Feeling your whole body in this relaxed state, and just focusing on how it feels with your gentle breathing.

Allowing your body to feel so relaxed it's becoming heavy. Sinking into the bed you are laying in.

Letting this meditation go. Letting this experience go.

As we end this meditation, just know that it is okay if it takes a little while longer to fall asleep, there is no rush. The point is to get your body into this wonderful relaxed state, and to just enjoy it. If you wish to continue this experience on your own, continue breathing at the tempo we mentioned before. I will lead you in six times and then I will stop talking, so you can continue it on your own. Before I begin, thank you for listening, and have a wonderful sleep.

Making sure you are breathing from the back of your throat, and also from your abdomen area:

Breathe in for four seconds.

Hold for four seconds.

Breathe out for six seconds.

Hold for two seconds.

Breathe in for four seconds.

Hold for four seconds.

Breathe out for six seconds.

Hold for two seconds.

Breathe in for four seconds.

Hold for four seconds.

Breathe out for six seconds.

Hold for two seconds.

Breathe in for four seconds.

Hold for four seconds.

Breathe out for six seconds.

Hold for two seconds.

Breathe in for four seconds.

Hold for four seconds.

Breathe out for six seconds.

Hold for two seconds.

Breathe in for four seconds.

Hold for four seconds.

Breathe out for six seconds.

Hold for two seconds.

Goodnight.

Guided Sleep Meditation | 60 Minutes | 875 Words

Hello and welcome to this guided meditation for sleep. Before we begin, make sure everything is ready for you to fall asleep. Set your alarm, tuck yourself in, and when you are ready, relax. Make sure you are in a comfortable position with your spine straight, and that your eyes are closed.

Breathing in, and out.

Relaxing your body, and letting go of your day.

Giving your body permission to relax.

Letting your breath move into your belly or your lower abdomen.

Letting go of your thoughts.

Letting go of your stress.

Letting go of any anxiety.

Letting go of any fears.

Letting go of your worries.

Letting go of any nerves or uncomfortable energy.

Letting go of everything.

Giving yourself permission here to enter a relaxed state, where everything is okay.

Feeling a sense of safety.

Feeling a sense of serenity.

Feeling a sense of tranquility and calmness flow into your body with each inhalation.

Breathing in.

Breathing out.

Breathing in.

Breathing out.

Breathing in.

Breathing out.

Taking a moment to listen to what your body needs right now.

Does it need relaxation?

Peace?

Love?

Security?

Serenity?

Warmth?

Energy?

Whatever it is, take a moment to build an intention.

Complete this sentence with whatever word you want, and say it either out loud or in your mind: "Tonight I fill my body with *blank* as I sleep."

Whatever word you chose, whether it was peace, relaxation, rest, or anything you wish, imagine that the beautiful energy of that word is beginning to surround you.

As if each inhalation you take brings that word closer into your body.

Each inhalation brings that word and the energy it contains into your lungs, into your body, into your blood, into your cells.

Releasing anything you no longer need on your exhalations.

Keeping your breath slow, languid, and deep.

Imagine that the word has a color forming, or a texture, or a sound as a representation as the word. Each time you breathe in the word, you breathe in even more of its energy. If it is showing up as a color, breathing in that color. If it is showing up as a sound, breathing in that sound.

Letting your imagination have fun.

Letting this word surround your body, cocooning you.

Letting this word swirl around your body, keeping you safe, keeping you loved, keeping you held.

Letting this word energetically tuck you in for a wonderful, relaxing sleep.

Letting your thoughts go even more.

Letting your day go even more.

Letting your life go even more.

Everything is okay.

Everything is safe.

It is okay to drift off... into a wonderful... relaxing... sleep.

Letting your breathing get rhythmically slower, gentler, deeper.

Letting your body feel relaxed, safe, and secure.

Breathing in that beautiful word…

Breathing out whatever you no longer need.

Everything is okay where you are.

It is okay for you to have wonderful sleep.

It is okay for you to wake up feeling deeply refreshed, rejuvenated, and inspired.

It is okay for you to detach from the world, have some "you-time" and give yourself attention.

It is okay for you to feel relaxed.

It is okay for you to feel happy.

Give yourself absolute permission to fall asleep now.

Knowing that you are worthy of having amazing, relaxing sleep.

You deserve to feel rejuvenated every morning.

You deserve to feel rested and alive.

You deserve beautiful, divine sleep.

Breathing slow, and deep.

Letting your beautiful word cocoon you in safety.

You are safe.

Letting your body go.

Letting all of your stress and tension go.

Letting all the little worries, fears, and concerns go.

Letting your responsibilities go.

Letting it all go.

Drifting off into peace.

Drifting off into sleep.

Drifting off into rejuvenating sleep.

Feeling your face relax.

Feeling your eyes relax.

Feeling your cheeks relax.

Feeling your scalp relax.

Feeling your jaw relax.

Feeling your tongue relax.

Feeling your mouth relax.

Feeling your neck relax.

Feeling your spine relax.

Feeling your shoulders relax.

Feeling your arms relax.

Feeling your hands relax.

Feeling your chest relax.

Feeling your back relax.

Feeling your waist relax.

Feeling your abs relax.

Feeling your hips relax.

Feeling your groin relax.

Feeling your buttocks relax.

Feeling your upper legs relax.

Feeling your lower legs relax.

Feeling your feet relax.

Feeling your whole body feel so relaxed.

Breathing in through your belly or lower abdomen.

Letting all your remaining tension go.

Letting yourself feel more relaxed than you have ever felt before.

Letting yourself feel more tranquil and serene than you have ever felt before.

Letting yourself feel more peaceful and calm than you have ever felt before.

Breathing into this wonderful body of yours and luxuriating in how calm and serene it feels.

Letting your breath feel fluid.

Letting your mind go.

Letting your body go.

Letting your emotions go.

Letting it all go.

Just slowly drifting off into the beautiful land of sleep.

Letting yourself just enjoy witnessing you falling asleep.

Letting yourself be where you are.

Breathing steadily, slowly, languidly.

This meditation will end soon. Continue breathing, and just enjoying this experience.

The body can rest deeply while you are still awake. Just the act of staying still, breathing, and letting it rest is still rejuvenating in itself.

Wherever you are in your drifting off process, have a lovely, rejuvenating, and refreshing night.

Thank you for listening.

Lunch Break Relaxation | 15 Minutes | 1221 Words

Hello and welcome to this fifteen minute guided meditation for lunch break relaxation. Here we will go into simple ways to relax your body and prepare you when you go back to work. Feel free to listen to this meditation as many times as you need. Each time you listen to it, you may notice a different experience. It is recommended to bring all of your attention to this meditation while listening to it and to not multitask. We will go through a few different ways to relax. If one of them resonates with you, you can simply repeat it throughout the day, even when you are at your desk. It may be interesting to note how your body feels now versus how it feels after this meditation.

Focusing on your breath is one of the easiest and quickest ways to relax the body while energizing it at the same time! As the body relaxes and becomes less overstimulated, that's where there is also a lot of calming practical energy that has endurance. Instead of finding energy fueled by stimulants and stress, there is another type of energy fueled by relaxation and peace. Let's explore some breathing exercises and feel this calming energy in your body.

Wherever you are, please take a moment to get comfortable. You can sit or lie down, but make sure your spine is straight.

Close your eyes and relax.

As you breathe, become present with the sensation of breathing.

Notice the physical sensations as you breathe in and out.

Notice the temperature. Feel the cool air entering your nose, warmed up by your throat, and the warm temperature as it reaches your lungs. Notice the warm air leaving your lungs, up your throat, and warm air exiting your nostrils.

Notice the gentle sensations as your chest and abdomen expand and contract with each breath.

Notice how each exhalation brings your body into a slightly deeper state of relaxation.

Being present with the sensations of your breath and how it affects your body.

Each breath can release a bit of pent up anxiety.

Each breath can release a bit of pent up stress.

Letting these heavy emotions go on your exhalations.

Breathing in and letting all your heavy emotions go. It could be fear, it could be fatigue, it could be worry, it could be stress. Whatever it is, letting it go on your exhalations to the best of your ability. Just enjoy the sensation of these heavy emotions leaving your body on your exhalations.

Letting any stress or anxiety begin to drip off of your body onto the floor where the Earth absorbs it. Releasing this on your exhalations.

Letting your fears drip onto the floor where the Earth absorbs it. Releasing this on your exhalations.

Letting all of your thoughts melt away from your mind into the Earth. Releasing this on your exhalations.

Letting them go. Perhaps they were never yours to begin with.

Perhaps letting a space or a silence begin to open up between your breaths. A pause or a moment.

Letting go of the need to "do" and embracing the ability to "be". Being here as you experience this meditation.

Letting go of any expectations you have.

Letting go of any conscious or unconscious judgements you may have of yourself.

Just being present with what is happening right now.

Enjoying the sensations of your breath.

Letting your body relax a bit more every moment.

Imagine that you are breathing in this light refreshing energy from above you now, and releasing out any stagnant energy. Having fun with this new imagery, perhaps imagining the light energy as a fun colour that you can breathe in.

Feeling this light entering all parts of your body.

Letting it swirl down into your body through the top of your head to your torso, and then your arms, and then your legs. Breathing in this light energy. Breathing out anything you wish to release. Letting the light be absorbed by your skin, your muscles, your bones, and all of the cells in your body.

Imagining that you could breathe through your legs and feet and absorb this light. Imagining that you could breathe through all the skin, muscles, bones, and cells.

Letting any stress, anxiety, tension or worry go on the exhalations. Breathing in this light through your breath into your legs and feet, and letting everything go on your exhalations.

Repeating this except through your whole torso now. Imagining that your lungs filled all parts of your torso. Breathing into every area, every cell, every organ, every part of you, and exhaling out. Repeating this for a little while.

Letting any stress, anxiety, tension or worry go on the exhalations. Breathing in this light through your breath into your torso, and letting everything go on your exhalations.

Moving to your arms and hands and breathing into here. Imagining that you could breathe through all the skin, muscles, bones, and cells.

You absorb the light as you breathe in, and release anything you no longer need on your exhalations.

And finally, breathing into your neck and head. Feeling your breath and this light affect all of your skin, muscles, bones, nerves and cells. Letting any stress, anxiety, tension or worry go on the exhalations. Breathing in this light through your breath into your neck and head, and letting everything go on the exhalation.

Now imagine that you could breathe through your whole body. Imagining that every part of your body was absorbing this light as you breathe into each cell.

Letting any stress, anxiety, tension or worry go on the exhalations. Breathing in this light through your breath into your body, and letting everything go on the exhalation.

Breathing at a pace that is comfortable for you.

Enjoying the sensations.

We're now going to ground this experience into your body so that when you return back to work you are able to integrate what has happened in a relaxed way.

Imagine as though your legs are like roots into the ground and your feet extend all the way into the Earth. You could imagine your legs are roots of a tree or a plant.

As you breathe through your body, your root-legs breathe in the Earth itself. Bringing this energy up your body, into your heart where it spreads to the rest of your body, your arms, your hands, and your head.

Breathing in this energy, breathing out into Earth.

Breathing in through your root-legs, breathing out.

When you are ready, take a moment to come back into your body. Wiggle your toes and feel the physical sensations again.

Wiggle your fingers and feel the physical sensations again.

Move your body a bit, perhaps take a nice stretch.

Open your eyes when you are ready.

When you are working you can continue any of the exercises described here. Perhaps while you are sitting at your desk you can imagine you are breathing in the light and exhaling out any tension. Perhaps you can imagine you are breathing in through the Earth. Whatever works best for you. Have fun with it, it is simply a tool that one can use to help balance energy levels at work, while maintaining focus for productivity.

Thank you so much for listening to this meditation. Have a wonderful rest of your day.

After Work Relaxation | 30 Minutes | 1885 Words

Hello and welcome to this thirty minute guided meditation for after work relaxation. Work is a wonderful thing. It provides us with monetary resources, a social network, a sense of purpose, but it can also sometimes be overwhelming, taxing, and stressful. Here we will go over some simple ways to relax after a long workday so that your personal time can be relaxing for your mind, heart and body.

Make sure you are comfortable as you sit or lie down and that your spine is straight. You may want to turn your electronic devices on to do not disturb for the duration of this meditation. It is recommended to bring all of your focus to this meditation and to not multitask.

Take a moment to settle in. When you are ready, close your eyes.

Imagine that all of your stress, fears, worry, and anxiety could just drift away from your mind like smoke on a breeze.

Imagine that any tension, fear, worry, or anxiety in your heart just melts away into the ground or the Earth beneath you.

Imagine that any heaviness, fatigue, worry, and anxiety in your body just fell off into the Earth.

Let go of anything you wish to release here.

Feeling any heaviness just fall off of you, or drift away.

See if you can breathe through your belly in slow deep breaths.

Simply bring your awareness to the sensation of breathing into your belly.

As if you were like a solar panel, imagine that the Earth's molten core was like a sun and you could absorb energy from it into your body. Your feet, legs, body, arms, hands, and head all absorb grounding, relaxing, and soothing energy from the Earth.

Imagine as if your legs were like roots that could go into the Earth and absorb its energy, perhaps reaching all the way down into the Earth's core.

Just breathe in as if you were absorbing the gentle, soothing energy of the Earth itself.

This energy is absorbed into your body and is relaxing any stressful thoughts, heavy feelings, or tense muscles that you have.

This energy provides you with relaxation and love, while taking away any stress or anxiety you carry.

Let your breath slow down.

Let time slow down.

It's just you and your connection to Earth.

In this moment in time, there are no fears, no worries, no pressures. It's just you and Earth.

Earth revitalizes and energizes you through your connection with it.

Any aches and pains in your body, Earth takes it away now.

Any fears in your mind, Earth takes it away now.

Letting Earth take all of your heaviness, and replace it with relaxing energy.

Almost as if Earth was a living entity that wanted to help your body in any way that it could.

As you breathe, using your imagination, perhaps you are smelling your favorite scents of Earth. Perhaps it is the scent of flowers in the summer heat, the scent of a lively forest, the scent of a burning fire, or whatever comes up naturally. Breathing in your favorite scent of Earth using your wonderful imagination.

As you listen, you now hear different sounds of earth. Perhaps you hear the sounds of trees swaying in the wind, the sounds of birds in the distance, the sounds of the ocean, the sounds of a waterfall, the sounds of a fire, or whatever comes up for you naturally. Using your imagination to hear your favorite sounds around you.

As you taste, you have the flavor of your favorite food on your tongue. Perhaps you taste your favorite fruit or vegetable, your favorite home cooked meal, the refreshing taste of pure clean water, or whatever comes up for you naturally.

As you feel your body, imagine you have the most wonderful sensations around you. Perhaps you're sitting in a hot tub, a cool refreshing pool or ocean, perhaps you're just resting somewhere peacefully in silence, perhaps you're out in nature with the wind on your skin and hair. Whatever comes up for you, using your imagination to feel your favorite physical sensations.

Imagine you could see your favorite environment around you. Have fun with this like a child again. Imagine that you were in a beautiful forest, a playground, near a volcano, a mountain, the ocean, whatever you wish.

Just letting these images float through your mind. Just have fun with it and let it happen naturally.

As you breathe continually feeling any heaviness, pain, fatigue, or stress being replaced with joy, happiness, and fulfillment.

Let's move your awareness to your emotions.

Is there any emotion you need right now? Happiness, joy, peace, fulfillment? You can ask Earth for it and Earth can send you the energy up through your roots into your body.

So what would you like to ask for from Earth?

Feel Earth give that to you now. Feel it being absorbed up through your feet, legs, your body, up into your arms and hands, up into your neck and head. Filling all parts of your body from your skin, to your muscles, to your bones, to your nerves, to your blood, to your organs, to every cell in your body. You are filled with the sensation of what you asked for.

Every inhalation brings in even more of this energy into your body.

Every exhalation pulls you deeper into what you asked for.

Feeling surrounded and filled with this wonderful emotion that you asked for.

Releasing this imagery when you are ready.

Connecting even deeper to Earth, just follow along with what I am suggesting and witness as your body becomes even more relaxed.

Bring your awareness to your feet. In just one moment, tense up all the muscles in your feet without hurting yourself and hold it for ten seconds. I will count down for you, and then you can release on an exhalation.

Tense up everything in your feet for ten, nine, eight, seven, six, five, four, three, two, one and release on an exhalation. Feeling your feet let everything go and relax.

Moving your awareness to your lower legs and all the muscles here. In one moment tense up these muscles to the best of your ability for ten seconds without hurting yourself.

Tense everything up for ten, nine, eight, seven, six, five, four, three, two, one and release on an exhalation. Letting your breath and your body relax. Feeling your lower legs feel so relaxed and wonderfully heavy now.

Moving to your upper legs. In one moment tightening up all the muscles in this area to the best of your ability for ten seconds. Don't hurt yourself, just feel the muscles contracting.

Tense up your upper legs for ten, nine, eight, seven, six, five, four, three, two, one and release on an exhalation. Feeling the relaxation of your upper legs now and how wonderfully heavy they feel.

Now moving up to your buttocks and groin area. This includes the muscles in your buttocks and the pelvic floor. In one moment tightening up this whole area in a contraction for ten seconds. Just doing the best you can here.

Tensing everything for ten, nine, eight, seven, six, five, four, three, two, one and release on an exhalation. Letting everything go and just taking a moment to enjoy the sensation of relaxation in this area.

Now your lower abdomen and lower back area.

Tensing up these muscles without hurting yourself for ten, nine, eight, seven, six, five, four, three, two, one and release on an exhalation. Letting everything go after, enjoying the relaxing sensations.

Now your upper abdomen and around to your back. Contracting this area to the best of your ability for ten second and breathing as you're doing this.

For ten, nine, eight, seven, six, five, four, three, two, one and release on an exhalation. Letting everything go and enjoying the relaxation after.

This area may feel funny to contract so just have fun with it. It includes your rib cage area, your chest muscles, and your upper back. It's okay if you leave a section out just do the best you can. Breathing in and contracting here for ten seconds.

Ten, nine, eight, seven, six, five, four, three, two, one and release on an exhalation. Letting everything go and relaxing this entire area. Enjoying the new sensations.

Now contracting your shoulder areas, including your shoulder blades. Breathing into here as you contract them for ten seconds.

Ten, nine, eight, seven, six, five, four, three, two, one and release on an exhalation. Letting everything go. Enjoying the new sensations of relaxation.

Bringing your awareness to your upper arms. Contracting here for ten seconds as you breathe. Doing the best you can and just enjoying it. Keeping your breathing going.

For ten, nine, eight, seven, six, five, four, three, two, one and release on an exhalation. Letting everything go and enjoying the new sensations of relaxation.

Focusing on your lower arms, feeling the sensation of contracting here for ten seconds. Tightening up the muscles as you breathe.

For ten, nine, eight, seven, six, five, four, three, two, one and release on an exhalation. Letting everything go and enjoying the relaxing sensations after.

Bringing your awareness to your hands, tightening up this entire area including all of your fingers and the palm of your hand for ten seconds as you breathe.

Ten, nine, eight, seven, six, five, four, three, two, one and release on an exhalation. Letting everything go. Enjoying the sensations of relaxation after.

Back up to your neck. Tensing up this area to the best of your ability without hurting yourself. Keep your breathing going as you do this.

For ten, nine, eight, seven, six, five, four, three, two, one and release on an exhalation. Letting everything go. Enjoying the sensations of relaxation after.

Up to your head now, in one moment scrunching up all of your face, pulling all of your muscle into a contraction and holding it for ten seconds. Tightening your jaw, your tongue, your cheeks, your forehead. Don't contract to the point of pain, just a tightening of the muscles.

For ten, nine, eight, seven, six, five, four, three, two, one and release on an exhalation. Letting everything go. Enjoying the new sensations of relaxation.

Now the whole body. Keep your breathing going as you tense up your whole body without hurting yourself for ten, nine, eight, seven, six, five, four, three, two, one and release on an exhalation.

Just sitting in this relaxation for a moment. Enjoying the sensations of relaxation.

Whenever you are ready, opening up your eyes and taking in the room you are in.

Taking in the sounds without judgement.

Taking in the scents of where you are.

Taking in the flavor and sensation of your tongue.

Taking in how your body feels.

Perhaps giving yourself a light stretch if it feels good for you to do that.

One last deep breath in, and letting it all go.

Thank you for listening to this meditation. You can listen to this meditation as many times as you need. The more you practice it, the more relaxing the results will be. This meditation will help relax you into a calming state so that you can enjoy the rest of your day in peace.

Have a relaxing day and goodbye.

Calm Yourself After a Panic Attack | 30 Minutes | Words 1557

Hello and welcome to this meditation dedicated to anyone who has recently had a panic attack and is still recovering from it. If you're experiencing one right now, it is best to call a hotline or a mental health professional as immediate help is best. This is to help soothe over the aftereffects of a panic attack.

Wherever you are, just take a moment to sit or lie down and get comfortable. If you are cold, it may be best to put a blanket over you to make sure you stay warm. Treat yourself as gently as if you were a little child right now.

Make sure you're in a safe environment, and whenever you feel ready to, close your eyes.

If there are any exercises you really liked during this meditation, you can repeat it throughout the day to keep yourself calm. It is also perfectly okay if you fall asleep during this meditation.

Just take one big breath in and out.

Another big breath in and out.

Everything is okay.

Put your hand over your heart and repeat these words either out loud or in your mind:

I am safe.

I love who I am.

I am loved.

I am worthy of a calm life.

I am worthy of feeling loved.

Love surrounds me everywhere I go.

My life is full of love, light, safety, and laughter.

You can put your hand down now and let's focus on your breath.

Breathing in and out and bit slower than you normally would.

Your breathing may be quite high in your chest right now, which is perfectly normal, but see if you can lower it down your torso as much as you can comfortably allow.

This means, if your breathing feels as if it's in your upper chest, just lower your breath to your rib cage area. As if you are breathing from a lower part of your body.

If your breath is in your rib cage area, see if you can lower it to the middle of your torso.

if it is in the middle of your torso, see if you can lower it into your belly.

If it is in your belly, see if you feel like you are breathing from the bottom of your torso.

Tiny steps are all that is needed to get strong effects from this meditation.

Allowing your breath to be a little bit slower than it usually would be, and allowing your breathing to be a little bit lower on your body than where it usually would be.

There's no rush to make it any slower or deeper than needed.

Just enjoying the sensations of breathing in, and out.

You may notice that your body, very slowly, begins to relax a bit.

Just note what is happening.

Breathing in, and out, at a pace that is soothing for you.

Keeping your breathing going.

Letting your breath very slowly calm down your body.

When you are in a panic attack your body goes into fight, flight, or freeze mode. It is exhausting for the body to go through, so you can also think of it like you just had a huge workout and you are in rest mode now. It is going to take some time for the adrenaline to be released, and for your body to be able to enter a relaxed state again. Take this as slowly as you need to, and just enjoy the process as much as you can.

Keeping your breath going.

If you want to curl over on to your side into the fetal position that is okay too, whatever makes your body feel safe.

Deepening your breath a little bit more in your body. Feeling what is best for you.

And beginning to let your body relax a bit more.

If you are ready to, bring your awareness to just one part of the body. Maybe you focus on your arms, or one foot, or your face, or your abs, and just breathe into that area. Take one area of the body, and relax just that area.

Breathing into here.

Letting any stress or anxiety go as much as you are comfortable with.

Every breath releases a tiny bit more stress.
Every breath releases a tiny bit more anxiety.

Every breath releases a tiny bit more tension from this area of your body.

Now take your awareness to another part of your body, right beside the part you just relaxed. If you relaxed one foot, focus on the ankle now. If you relaxed an arm, focus on the shoulder. Just something small nearby. Breathe into that area now.

On the exhalations let go of anything you feel safe to release.

Now move to one more part of the body nearby. If you were calming down your neck, now move to your chest. If you were calming down part of your leg, now move to the hips. Let the area be a little bit bigger if you are comfortable with that.

Breathing into here, and letting all of the stress and anxiety go on the exhalation.

Breathing in, and releasing all of your stress.

Seeing now if you can deepen your breath a bit more.

Seeing if you can lower your breath into your body a bit more. If it is still in your chest, just lowering it down into your abdomen. Again, only doing what feels best for your body. There is no rush. Slower is better.

Seeing if you can now calm down one more part of the body. The same thing as before, being very slow and gentle with this.

Breathing into the area, and releasing any tension on the exhalation.

If you are getting overwhelmed, just continually focus one one part of the body alone.

Deepening your breathing even more if possible. A little slower, a little more calm.

If you feel ready, see if you can connect to the entirety of your body, and imagine that you are breathing into your whole body, and exhaling all the tension and stress through your whole body. Breathing into your body, and exhaling out anything that's needed. Feeling as though your whole body can participate in every breath in and every breath out.

If you cannot do this, simply focus on one body part, there is no right or wrong here.

Breathing deeply, steadily, and enjoying the sensations if possible.

Staying here for a while longer. Breathing into your whole body- or just one part of your body if needed.

Letting your breath settle on a tempo that feels best for you.

Imagine that your body is building beautiful roots from it into the ground beneath you. Imagine that you are a beautiful plant or tree that can absorb nutrients from Earth from these roots.

These roots spread from any part of your body into the Earth and instantly create this calm, soothing energy for you.

Earth is calming to connect to, and you can absorb Earth's soothing energy right through these roots, into your body.

Your roots can go as far down into the Earth as you desire.

Breathing in Earth's calming nutrients into your body, and exhaling out any remaining tension.

Spreading your roots deeper and deeper into Earth, as far down as you wish.

You may decide to spread your roots all the way into Earth's core, feeling a warmth and love there. Sometimes it is best to just keep your roots on the crust of the earth, stabilizing your body. Any choice is the correct choice for you.

Breathing in Earth's energy into your body, and exhaling out any remaining tension.

Now for anyone who wishes to, you can imagine that your body is so deeply connected to Earth, that when you breathe you are breathing through Earth itself. Your lungs are Earth's lungs. You are breathing as Earth.

Each inhalation fills up all of Earth.

Each exhalation is released through Earth.

Just do this to the degree that you feel comfortable with.

Breathing in as if you and Earth are one.

Breathing out as if you and Earth are one.

Letting each breath pull you deeper and deeper into the calming energy of Earth.

Letting your breathing slow down a bit more if it feels comfortable to do so.

Breathing in as Earth, and breathing out as Earth.

We're going to gently come back into your body now.

Slowly come back into the sensations of your body.

Notice the sensations of gravity on your body.

Notice the feeling of fabric on your skin.

Notice the temperature of where you are.

Notice the surrounding sounds.

Notice the surrounding scents.

Notice the taste in your mouth, any flavours you notice.

Slowly open your eyes and take in the light. Notice the colours. Notice any shapes.

Take one big stretch if you wish to. Stretch all parts of your body.

Thank you for listening to this meditation. For the rest of your day, it is recommended to be very gentle with yourself. Could you treat yourself as if you accepted and loved all parts of you? Would you push someone who has gone through something very emotionally and physically draining to be at their peak productivity today? Perhaps not. Just let yourself be where you are, give yourself permission to move slowly, and take the time to love who you are.

Quick Relaxation Through Visualization | 15 Minutes | 1184 Words

Hello and welcome to this guided meditation for a quick relaxation session using visualization. If you have a busy schedule and you struggle to find the time to meditate, this will help fit in a soothing meditation so you can get back to your daily activities with ease. It is recommended to once in a while listen to a longer meditation so that your body can experience deeper levels of relaxation. Perhaps listening to one as you are falling asleep so that it doesn't take up any extra time. Relaxation is kind of like a habit or mentality that is built over time. A daily practice of meditation for your mind, body, and emotions can eventually cause your average life experience to be more peaceful. This means that when stressful things pop up in your life, or responsibilities pile up, you are able to choose the state you want to remain in rather than reacting to what is going on externally. It allows for greater productivity, happiness, and peace.

Let's begin. Make sure you're in a comfortable position and that you won't be disturbed for the next fifteen minutes. You may want to close the door to the room you are in, and turn your electronics on to do not disturb.

When you are comfortable, take some time to settle in. Close your eyes when you are ready.

Imagine there is a ball in front of you. It's filled with swirling colors, lights, and energy.

This ball contains all of your stress, responsibilities, duties, worries, anxieties, and anything you wish to let go of. It does not matter what is in here, it is just filled with what you want to release.

Allow this ball that is filled with heavy energy to grow as large as you wish. Once it has grown to the full size that feels right to you, say either out loud or in your mind "I release you for the next fifteen minutes."

You can imagine that this ball burns away in fire, floats up into the clouds, is washed away by water, or drifts down into the Earth. Whatever works best.

Now, you are just left with you.

Bring your awareness to your abdomen. Breathe into this area. Feel the sensation as your breath fills your abdomen, and the sensation as your breath leaves your abdomen.

Allow your breath to flow through your body at a pace that feels right for you.

Feeling the sensation of air expanding your abdomen.

And the sensation as your abdomen contracts when you exhale.

Imagine that above you there are beautiful clouds that are forming. They can be whatever colour you wish. Perhaps a bright blue, perhaps a gentle pink, perhaps a deep green.

A gentle rain begins to shower down upon you. Its temperature is perfect, not too cold, not too warm, just right.

It smells like the most beautiful scent. It could be flowers, it could be the ocean breeze, whatever arises for you.

The rain has a distinct color. You might see crystal raindrops, refracting all the colors of the rainbow. You might see forest green rain. You might see bright blue rain. You might see deep purple rain. Just pick what resonates with you the most.

The sound as it hits your body sounds like a beautiful melody quietly playing. Gently lulling your mind into relaxation.

As the rain touches your body it kisses your skin with the perfect temperature, sensation, and feeling. Almost as if your body is being cocooned by water.

As this rain moves over your body you notice it takes away all the stress, pain, tension, worry, anxiety, or unpleasant emotions you may wish to release.

As it washes over you with its gentle raindrops it takes with it all of this pain, and then drips down into the Earth beneath you, away from your body.

It just gently flows down your body into the Earth, taking anything you no longer need with it.

It sort of feels like you're at the bottom of a gentle waterfall.

As you breathe in, you smell the beautiful scent of the rain. The healing scents move into your body all the way into your abdomen, and take any heaviness with it on the exhalations.

The sounds lull your mind into relaxation.

The feeling of the rain is so soothing. It's the perfect temperature. It's so safe feeling.

The colour is beautiful.

If you wanted to taste the rain, it also has the freshest taste. Perhaps a bit like fruit. Perhaps like the purest spring water you have ever tried. Whatever comes up for you.

Breathing in deeply as you experience this. A gentle inhalation and exhalation at a pace that feels right for your body right now.

Letting this experience wash away any thoughts you no longer wish to have.

Letting this experience wash away any emotions you no longer want to hold on to.

Letting this experience wash away any pain or tension in your body that you no longer want to experience.

Letting it all go with the rain flowing down your body.

Breathing in this experience, and letting everything go on your exhalations.

Letting this rain wash over you and take anything you are willing to release.

Feeling the flow of water down your skin.

Hearing the sounds of the rain. Perhaps with a beautiful melody with each water drop, perhaps not, whatever you hear is perfect for you.

Smelling the beautiful scents of the rain.

Tasting the rain if you wish to.

Seeing the rain and its beautiful colors or crystal clarity.

Letting everything go.

Having all of your tension and pain just melting away from you into the Earth.

Giving this rain permission to take away what you no longer need.

Breathing from your abdomen as you do this. Letting your breath be rhythmic and slow.

Feeling your body relax.

Feeling your mind let go.

Feeling your emotions balance out into peace and tranquility.

Enjoying this experience, just as you are.

Keeping your breathing going.

Knowing this rain is here just for you and no one else. It has been specifically made to help heal you. Let your body release whatever it is willing to release.

When you are ready, gently letting go of this experience. Knowing that the rain will be here for you whenever you want to experience it again.

Wiggling your fingers and toes when you are ready Feeling the wonderful sensations come back into those areas.

Perhaps taking a light stretch.

Feeling how your body is now.

Noting any scents in the room.

Hearing any surrounding sounds.

Tasting the natural flavor on your tongue right now.

Opening your eyes when you feel ready.

Regarding the swirling ball of emotions you released in the beginning of this meditation, you can either permanently let it go now, or you can call it back.

To let it go, just don't call it back.

To call it back, have it re-enter your heart again.

I wish you a wonderful and peaceful rest of your day. Thank you for listening to this meditation. Goodbye.

Affirmations for Deep Healing | 30 Minutes | 1115 Words

Hello and welcome to this meditation for deep healing. In this guided meditation we will be focusing on affirmations. It is recommended to follow along as if you could feel these words in your physical body, and not just saying it verbatim. Affirmations are not just about the words being said, they are about what the words represent. Find a way to bring your emotions and your body into believing that these affirmations are true, and that's when the results will begin to form. Affirmations are not a magical tool. It is still necessary to do the work to get what you are aiming for. However, it will bring your mind, body, and emotions into believing that you already have it, and therefore it will be a lot easier to accomplish. It's like giving yourself a goal through affirmations, versus trying to get somewhere using your old habits that caused the problem in the first place.

Please take some time to sit or lie down in a comfortable position.

Make sure your spine is straight, and that you can comfortably remain here for the next thirty minutes.

It is recommended to turn your phone on to do not disturb, and to bring your total awareness to this meditation and not multitask while listening to this.

Let your body have a moment to relax.

Enjoy the silence.

Let your breath naturally slow down.

Let go of any responsibilities.

Bring your awareness into the present moment.

Breathe in and out.

In and out.

Continue at a pace comfortable for you.

Let it all go.

Let your day go.

Let yourself go.

Relax.

Repeat these words either in your mind or out loud. See if you can feel it in your body:

I am healthy in all ways.

I am loved in all ways.

I am abundant in all ways.

My body, my mind, my emotions, and my soul all work in harmony.

My life is full of health and vitality.

I have wonderful high energy levels.

My immune system is strong and healthy.

My nutrition and diet is strong and healthy.

I make sure to feed my body nourishing foods.

My body has excellent digestion.

I have a wonderful relationship with my body.

My body and I respect each other and our needs.

I take care of my body as if it were my own child.

I love my body deeply.

I love all parts of my body.

I love my mind.

I love my intellect.

My intellect keeps me healthy and strong.

My mind is clear and serene.

My mind and I work together.

My mind and I are friends.

My mind, my body, my emotions, and my soul all work in harmony.

I love my emotions.

My emotions are balanced, regular, and calm.

My emotions are enriching and calming.

I allow myself to feel my emotions, which allows me to feel positive emotions.

I have a balanced emotional life.

I respect my emotions and honor them.

I know that honoring my emotions is a sign of intelligence.

I have an extremely high emotional IQ.

My emotions and I work together.

My emotions, my mind, my body, and my soul all work in harmony.

I love my energy.

My energy and I work together.

I have an excellent relationship with my essence and my personal energy.

I understand what my energy is as an individual person.

I understand what my energy is in a group of people.

My energy is authentically me.

I allow my true essence and energy to shine through.

I protect my energy while letting it speak.

I lovingly parent my energy, while giving it room to play.

I live a life that allows my true authenticity to be present.

My soul, my emotions, my body, and my mind all work together in harmony.

I am deeply healthy.

All parts of my health are balanced.

All parts of my life feel fulfilled.

I have a fulfilling, healthy life.

Stopping these affirmations, simply notice how your body feels now compared to how it felt before.

Take time to note any differences.

Notice if any parts of you feel lighter, or happier.

Notice if any parts of you feel different emotionally.

Notice if any parts of your mind feel a little more calm and relaxed.

If your eyes are not closed, I recommend closing them now.

Take a deep breath in and let everything go.

Using your imagination, see if you can mentally picture what your life would be like if you felt this way every single day.

How old are you?

Where are you?

What are you wearing?

What is your fitness level?

What is your flexibility level?

How happy do you feel?

What is the expression on your face?

Who is in your life?

What are you doing with your time throughout the day?

How do you spend your time?

What are you grateful for in this part of your life?

What brings a smile to your face in this part of your life?

Could you get here?

What would it take for you to get here?

Would you be willing to do it?

Would you be willing to take tiny steps each day to get closer to this destination?

If it naturally happens, is there anything that this future version of you would tell yourself right now? Any words of wisdom, or messages to share?

What about this future version of you is different from where you are right now?

Letting go of your future self in your imagination, bring your awareness to who you are right now listening to this meditation. Your current self.

What are you proud of about yourself?

What do you feel happy about, regarding who you are?

What are you thankful for about yourself?

What about yourself makes you feel healthy?

And just taking a moment to breathe.

Come back into your body.

Feel your feet. Breathe into them. Perhaps wiggle your toes.

Feel your legs. Perhaps stretch them.

Feel your torso. Breathe into here, perhaps take a gentle stretch.

Feel your arms. Breathe into here, perhaps stretch your arms.

Feel your neck and head. Breathe into here.

Feel the way your body is right now in relaxation.

Notice any smells where you are.

Notice any sounds.

Notice any flavors on your tongue.

When you are ready, open your eyes.

Slowly notice any colors.

Any shapes.

Any objects.

Taking one deep breath.

Thank you for participating in this guided meditation. The more you listen to this meditation, the more powerful it will be. You may find that each time you listen to it you have a completely different experience.

Have a wonderful day, and goodbye for now.

Deep Healing | 60 Minutes | 2632 Words

Welcome to this meditation designed for deep healing. In this meditation we will be exploring deep healing through your physical, mental, emotional, and spiritual experiences. If while listening to this meditation things become too uncomfortable for you, simply focus on your breath. Only you know what's best for your specific needs. This is just a guide to follow.

You may want to put your cell phone or electronics onto do not disturb so that any alerts that pop up do not distract you from this meditation.

Either sit or lie down in a comfortable position. Make sure your spine is straight. Give yourself a moment to settle your body down. If you feel cold take a moment to grab a blanket and put it over your body.

It is perfectly okay if you fall asleep during this meditation. Listen to your body.

Let's bring your conscious awareness to your breath.

Breathe at a pace that feels relaxing for you. Perhaps it is a little slower than usual, or a little lower in your body than usual, but follow what feels best for you. There is no right or wrong way to breathe, we're just focusing on slowing it down a little bit at a time.

Let go of any responsibilities you may feel looming over your shoulders. Let go of any to do lists, concerns, worries, or thoughts for the next hour. It is okay to take the time to focus on yourself. It is okay to put yourself first during this meditation.

Let go of any labels you may have given yourself unconsciously: your gender, your height, your country of origin, your political beliefs, your religious beliefs, your role within your family, your reputation in society….

Let go of who you think you are.

Let go of where you are.

Let go of what you are- whatever that means for you.

Let go of everything that you wish to release right now.

Using your breath to help you release everything. Breathing in.

Allowing your exhalations to let everything go.

You may find your exhalations are longer than your inhalations as you release everything.

Let the exhalation be as long as you are comfortable with.

Noticing how your body changes as you continue to breathe and let go of everything.

Continuing to let everything go.

Continuing to breathe deeply.

Continuing to relax.

Bring your awareness to your feet. On each exhalation, imagine your feet gently melting into the Earth itself.

Imagine the sensation of them being so relaxed with your breath, it feels as though they just melt into the Earth.

All of your muscles, stress, and tension melt away, until all that remains is the sensation of relaxation in your feet.

Stay with your feet for a little while, enjoying the sensation of relaxation here.

Bring your awareness to your ankles. Breathe into here steadily and slowly. On the exhalations feel the sensation of your ankles just melt into the Earth itself. Letting everything go, until all that remains is a feeling of relaxation.

Move your awareness up into your lower legs. Feel the strain, stress, or tension melt away into Earth. Let your lower legs feel so relaxed on the exhalations of your breathing. Letting everything go, until all that remains is a feeling of relaxation.

Move your awareness to your knees. Let all the different parts of your knee relax and melt into Earth. Let any pain, tightness, or tension go, until all that remains is a feeling of relaxation.

Move your awareness to your upper legs. Let all the stress and heaviness in your upper legs go. Feel it melt away into Earth. Letting everything go, until all that remains is a feeling of relaxation.

Keep your exhalations deep and relaxing. Seeing if you can just enjoy this experience.

Move your awareness to your hips. Feel this area melt into Earth. Feel all the tension, pain, and stiffness melt away from you. Letting everything go, until all that remains is a feeling of relaxation.

Move your awareness to your groin area. Breathe into here, feel any sensations that you do not need release into Earth. Feel it melt away from you. Letting everything go, until all that remains is a feeling of relaxation.

Move your awareness to your buttocks area. Breathe into here, and on the exhalations letting any sensations you do not need melt away from you into Earth, until all that remains is a feeling of relaxation.

Move your awareness to your lower abdomen and lower back area. Feel all the muscles, tension, or pain if there is any, melt away from your body into Earth. Feel all of it leave your body forever, until all that remains is a feeling of relaxation.

Move your awareness to your waist and the middle of your torso. Breathe into here, and on the exhalation letting any tension go. Enjoy the sensation as it melts into Earth until all that remains is a feeling of relaxation.

Making sure your breath remains slow and steady.

Move your awareness to your chest and upper back. Breathe into here, and on the exhalation let all of the tension or stress go. Let it melt into

Earth. Letting everything go, until all that remains is a feeling of relaxation.

Bring your awareness into your shoulder blades, shoulders, and armpits. Breathe into here. Let it all go. Let all the tension, stress, or heavy sensations go and witness as they melt into Earth on your exhalations. Continue until all that remains is a feeling of relaxation.

Just enjoy this experience.

Bring your awareness to your upper arms. Breathing into here, and on the exhalations letting everything go, until all that remains is a feeling of relaxation.

Feeling any tension in your elbows go. Just witnessing it melt away with your exhalations. Letting everything go, until all that remains is a feeling of relaxation.

Feeling any tension, strain, or heaviness go in the lower arms with your exhalations. Breathing in, and on your exhalations letting everything go, until all that remains is a feeling of relaxation.

Feeling any stress or pain released in your hands and wrists with your exhalations. Letting this area just melt into Earth. Letting everything go, until all that remains is a feeling of relaxation.

Coming up to your neck. Breathing into here and letting it all go with your exhalations. Letting all the tension and fatigue melt away into Earth, until all that remains is a feeling of relaxation.

Letting your face relax deeply. Feeling all the muscles melt away into Earth, until all that remains is a feeling of relaxation.

Letting your head and skull relax fully. All the tiny muscles here. All the tension here. Just feeling it melt into Earth, until all that remains is a feeling of relaxation.

Witnessing how different your body feels now. Letting it get even more relaxed with each breath.

Bringing your awareness to the thoughts in your mind.

Keeping your breathing slow and steady, and your body deeply relaxed.

Noticing any thoughts that pop up, and on your exhalations letting these thoughts go.

You can imagine that they drift away like smoke in a breeze, or like a balloon up into the air. Anything that allows you to experience them drifting away peacefully.

Noticing any thoughts, and just letting them drift away.

Breathing deeply.

Relaxing your body.

Noticing the mind.

Noticing if the pause between your thoughts becomes a little bit longer with each passing minute.

Accepting any thought that comes in, and releasing it.

Accepting where you are. It is okay if there are a lot of thoughts.

Breathing in, and just releasing any thoughts.

Allowing your mind to let everything go.

Allowing it to feel empty, relaxed and calm to the best of your ability.

Simply noting any thoughts that pop up, and gently releasing them.

Breathing in and out.

Relaxing the body.

Noticing the thoughts and releasing them.

Imagining that cool relaxing air is entering your mind now on every inhalation, and on the exhalation any heaviness or remaining clutter is released.

Breathing in cooling refreshing air… and releasing any heavy or cluttering thoughts on your exhalation.

Rejuvenating your mind into simple clarity.

Breathing in cooling light and energy, and breathing out anything you no longer need.

Letting your breath remain slow and gentle.

Let's bring your awareness to your emotions.

If you could notice your emotions right now, what do they feel like?

Do they feel heavy? Or light? It is okay if you cannot tell.

Do they feel easily accessible to you? Or is feeling your emotions a confusing concept?

Any answer is okay. We are going to do a very light healing exercise on your emotions. If you cannot feel anything during this part of the meditation, that is fine, just imagine it is working somewhere inside of you and relax.

Imagine that your emotions were as tangible as your physical sensations. When you feel happy your body lights up. When you feel sad your body pulls down. When you are confused, everything is jumping in new directions. It's like energy flowing through your body.

Imagine that you could breathe calming, soothing energy into your emotional body.

This calming energy is all around you. It has no real look to it, you can just feel it. As you breathe in, soothing energy fills and replaces all of your other emotions for the time being.

Any emotion feeling fear, feeling sadness, feeling anxiety, or anything uncomfortable is temporarily being replaced with this calming energy. We are not bulldozing over any emotions, just temporarily breathing in calming energy. Giving your emotional body a loving break.

As you exhale, you can release any fear, stress, anxiety, worry or any other emotions you wish to release.

Breathing in calming energy, and exhaling out any emotions you wish to release.

Just releasing as much as you are comfortable with, there's no need to push yourself.

Letting it happen naturally and effortlessly.

Taking a moment to release all of your heavy emotions and just enjoying the sensation of calmness in your emotional body.

Enjoying the sensation of breathing.

Enjoying the relaxation of your body.

Enjoying the silence of your mind.

Enjoying the peace of your emotions.

When you are ready, imagine that there is a beautiful ball of white light way above you.

It could feel like the light of creation, or it could feel just like a massive white light. Follow what concept feels best for your heart.

This white light above you has eternal, healing energy to give to you. It can soothe you, invigorate you, love you, heal you, whatever you need.

Ask this light for anything.

For example: "I need love," or "I need warmth". If you don't know, that's okay too, just follow along.

Feel this beautiful light shine down its white rays and caress your body with its love, feeding you whatever you need like you are a baby to this mother energy.

It fills up your body, your mind, your emotions, and your entire energy with this light.

Every part of you is cocooned in this beautiful energy.

Breathing in light all around you, and breathing out slowly.

Breathing in the light, and breathing out slowly.

Filling your body, your mind, your emotions, and your energy with this beautiful light.

Letting this light fill your toes.

Letting this light fill your feet.

Letting this light fill your ankles.

Letting this light fill your lower legs.

Letting this light fill your knees.

Letting this light fill your upper legs.

Letting this light fill your hips.

Letting this light fill your groin.

Letting this light fill your buttocks.

Letting this light fill your spine.

Letting this light fill your lower back.

Letting this light fill your lower abdomen.

Letting this light fill your waist.

Letting this light fill your mid back.

Letting this light fill the middle of your abdomen.

Letting this light fill all of your internal organs near your belly.

Letting this light fill your chest.

Letting this light fill your upper back.

Letting this light fill your ribcage and all of its internal organs.

Letting this light fill your heart.

Letting this light fill your lungs.

Letting this light fill your shoulder blades.

Letting this light fill your shoulders and armpits.

Letting this light fill your upper arms.

Letting this light fill your elbows.

Letting this light fill your lower arms.

Letting this light fill your wrists.

Letting this light fill your hands.

Letting this light fill your fingers.

Letting this light fill your neck.

Letting this light fill your jaw.

Letting this light fill your cheeks.

Letting this light fill your mouth.

Letting this light fill your nose.

Letting this light fill your eyes.

Letting this light fill your forehead.

Letting this light fill your hair.

Letting this light fill your scalp.

Letting this light fill your brain.

Letting this light flow through your whole body.

Breathing in this beautiful light and breathing out this beautiful light.

Just maintaining this connection for a little while. I'm going to go silent for a bit as you breathe in and out with this energy of light.

You can keep this connection to the light, but we are now going to do something called grounding to gently come out of this meditation. Being in the light feels wonderful, but it is equally as important to connect back to Earth so that it is a stable connection.

Imagining now, keeping your breath slow and steady, that Earth had a sun within itself too. It can be whatever colour you wish. It can look like the molten movement of the Earth's core, or perhaps like a beautiful green sun. Let your imagination have fun with this. There is no right or wrong.

This beautiful sun within the Earth, similar to the light above, shines up to you from inside the Earth and gives you anything you need: warmth, compassion, energy, relaxation.

Just breathe in this energy from the Earth.

Keeping your breathing slow and steady.

Letting this energy from the Earth be absorbed by your body. Letting the Earth's sun tendril up into your mind, body and emotions.

Breathing in the light from the Earth.

Exhaling out slowly.

Letting your body feel deeply tethered and connected to the Earth.

Perhaps you feel roots growing out of your body to connect to the Earth even more.

Perhaps you feel an umbilical cord to the earth to connect you even more.

Whatever comes up in your imaginative mind, just go with that.

Breathing in the Earth's energy.

Exhaling out slowly and gently.

Feeling the weight of gravity hugging you to the Earth.

Feeling how heavy your body is.

Feeling the touch of fabric and clothing on your skin.

Feeling the temperature of your body.

Noticing how your body feels physically.

Noticing any sounds around you. Paying attention to them without getting attached. Simply noticing the sounds.

Noticing any scents around you. Smelling the surrounding area. Just noticing it without judgement.

Noticing any flavors on your tongue. Perhaps from a past meal, perhaps from something you just drank. Being present with the flavor or sensation of your mouth.

Whenever you are ready, opening your eyes, and just taking in your surrounding environment. Taking in the colors. Taking in the light and shadows. Taking in the scenery. Being present with it all. Detached but here.

And simply repeat these three sentences after I say it, either out loud or in your mind:

I am healthy in all ways.

Every day in every way my body is becoming healthier and healthier.

I respect my body, and give it what it is asking for.

Thank you for listening to this meditation. Make sure to hydrate well today and get a good sleep tonight.

Recharge Your Energy | 30 Minutes | Words 2237

Hello and welcome to this meditation for recharging your energy in thirty minutes. Please make sure your full attention is on this guided meditation and you are not driving or operating machinery during this time. Allow yourself to get comfortable where you can sit or lay down for the next thirty minutes. Consider turning your electronic devices on to do not disturb.

Take a moment to bring your awareness to your body.

Notice how your body feels today.

Do you feel tired or full of energy?

Do you feel stiff or relaxed?

Do you feel hungry or content?

Do you feel thirsty or quenched?

Whatever you feel, just noting it to yourself.

Bringing your awareness to your breath. Just noting where it is.

Does it feel deep or shallow?

Does it feel slow or fast?

There is no need to change anything, just noticing what is going on.

Bringing your awareness to your mind.

Does your mind feel fast or slow?

Does your mind feel full of movement or slow and silent?

Noticing what is happening without judgement.

Bringing your awareness to your emotions. Just noticing how you feel here.

Do you feel sad or happy?

Do you feel angry or relaxed?

Do you feel fearful or full of peace?

Again, we are just noticing what we feel. There is no need to adjust anything.

There is no right or wrong answer to any of these questions, it is purely for your own benefit to build a relationship to the different sides of your personal experience.

At the end of the meditation we will come back to this exercise, so whatever you noted just now, take a moment to release it all. Letting it go.

What brought you to this meditation today?

How often are you in need of more energy, vitality, and love for yourself?

Energy is just like a current. When we eat food we allow our body to participate the current of physical energy. We eat nutritious food and absorb energy in, and then we expend energy out through activity.

Many of us don't realize there is a spiritual energy that we can tap into twenty-four seven that can provide us with mental, emotional, and physical energy.

Let's tap into it now.

Take a moment to deepen your breathing into a comfortable but slow state.

If you feel okay to try it, let your exhalations be a little longer than your inhalations.

Perhaps even let there be a pause between your inhalations and exhalations.

Only do what feels comfortable to you. It should not feel straining but relaxing and soothing.

At the very top of your head there is a chakra. This chakra is a connection to the spiritual energy mentioned before. Just imagine, or feel, that the top of your head is like a beautiful flower. It opens up to the degree that you are comfortable with to an imaginary light above you.

This flower is a representation of how much energy you can receive and it connects with this ray of light above.

This light above can come in many colors, red, purple, green, white, or whatever else you wish, but I will just call it gold for this exercise.

Feeling this golden light from above, gently cascading down, and caressing the flower on the top of your head.

Keeping your breath slow and relaxed. Imagine that you can feel its warmth, its love, and its generosity caressing the petals of your flower.

Whenever you feel ready, allow your flower to absorb this beautiful golden light.

This golden light enters through to the top of your head, into your skull. You can feel its gentle warmth.

It fills your brain, your eyes, your sinuses, your nostrils, your skull, your mouth, and it is even absorbed by your hair.

Every part of your head is basking in this light. Breathe it in, and as you breathe out release anything you wish to release.

This beautiful light gently moves down to your neck. You feel yourself breathing in this light. Feeling the gentle warmth, or the refreshing coolness of this energy. You feel it touching your vocal cords, the top of your spine, filling all of your beautiful skin, even energizing your blood cells in a loving way. All parts of your neck from the bones to the skin are receiving this light, and basking in it.

Breathe in this light, and on your exhalation release anything you wish to let go of.

This wonderful light moves down your body and is absorbed by your shoulders and collarbone area. Breathe in as you feel it filling the bones, the muscles, the ligaments, the tendons, the skin, and all parts of this area. On your exhalations releasing anything you no longer need.

This light flows down into your upper arms. Feeling this light being absorbed by your skin, your muscles, your bones, your blood cells, and all parts of your upper arm. Breathing in this light, and on the exhalations releasing anything you no longer need.

Now moving to your elbows. Feeling this light gently warming up and loving the tendons, the nerves, the bones, the cartilage, the skin. Breathing in this light, and exhaling out anything you no longer wish to hold on to.

Moving into your lower arms. Feeling this beautiful light being absorbed by your bones, the cells of your body here, all parts of your lower arm. Breathing in this light and exhaling out anything you no longer wish to hold on to.

Feeling this rejuvenating light pour into your beautiful hands. Filling each bone, each muscle, each vein, all of your skin, even your fingernails. Breathing in this light and exhaling out anything you no longer wish to hold on to.

Letting this light continue pouring down your body in a gentle but slow way. Moving from the crown of your head to your shoulders and arms, and down to your upper chest area. This includes your chest muscles, pecks or breasts, and around the upper ribcage to the upper back including your shoulder blades. Feeling this light being absorbed by your muscles, your bones, your nerves, your spine, your lungs, and your heart. Breathing in the light and exhaling out anything you no longer wish to hold on to.

Feeling this light move down to the middle of your torso. This includes the middle of your ribcage down to your waist, and your upper middle back. Just breathing into this area, as you feel the light soothing all parts of your body. Your ribcage, your spine, your lungs, your spleen, your stomach, your liver, your pancreas, your gallbladder, the bottom of your lungs, your muscles, your spine, and all cells of your body.

Breathing into here, and letting go of anything you no longer wish to hold onto.

It may begin to feel like you're being lit up from the inside out.

Just allowing any sensations to pass through you. Noting it and letting it go.

Keeping your breathing slow and steady.

There is no wrong way to do this, just do what feels best for you.

Allowing this healing, rejuvenating light to move down into your lower torso area. This includes your belly, your hips, and your lower back. Breathing into this area as you feel the light cascade and heal your skin, your blood, your bones, your intestines, your muscles, and all of your cells here. Releasing anything you no longer need on your exhalations.

Keeping your breath slow and steady. Allowing this energy to flow from the top of your head all the way down your body.

Allowing this light to move down your body into your lower torso, your groin, and your buttocks. Allowing this light to heal and be gently absorbed by all of your skin, all of your muscles, your reproductive organs, your blood, your nerves, and all of your cells here. Breathing in this light and exhaling anything you need to release here.

Letting this light move down into your upper legs. Filling your powerful muscles, tendons, ligaments, bones, veins, arteries, nerves, and all parts of your wonderful upper legs. Breathing in the light to your upper legs, and exhaling out anything you wish to release.

Letting this light move down into your knees. Filling the cartilage, all the intricate parts here, the gentle muscles, the ligaments, the tendons, and anything else you feel needs this light for healing. Breathing in the light, and exhaling out anything you no longer wish to hold on to.

Moving down into your lower legs. Filling your muscles, your bones, your veins and arteries, your nerves, your skin, all parts of your lower leg. Breathing in this light, and exhaling out anything you no longer wish to hold on to.

Feeling the light move down to your ankles and feet. Letting this light pool into here and light it up from the inside out. Filling all the bones, all the muscles, all the nerves, all the blood, all the intricate ligaments, the tendons, the joints, the skin, and even your toenails. Breathing into here, and letting anything you no longer wish to hold on to on your exhalations.

Letting this energy flow past your feet into the Earth beneath you. Kind of like you are in a current of this beautiful light above as it connects deep into the Earth beneath you.

Feeling this cascading light flowing down all parts of your body into the Earth.

Breathing in the light, letting it fill your lungs, and letting out any energy, thoughts, or sensations you wish to release.

Breathing in the light, and releasing whatever you wish to let go of on your exhalations.

Letting your breath evolve into a tempo that feels best for you. It may slow down a bit, it may speed up a bit, whatever feels best. Let your breath be an organic rhythm that can change as needed.

Remaining in that beautiful current of light from the flower at the top of your head, all the way down to your legs that are like roots into the Earth beneath you.

Let's come back to the same questions we asked in the beginning. Just note any changes.

Do you feel tired or full of energy?

Do you feel stiff or relaxed?

Do you feel hungry or content?

Do you feel thirsty or quenched?

Whatever you feel, just noting it to yourself.

Bringing your awareness to your breath now. Just noticing where it is.

Does it feel deep or shallow?

Does it feel slow or fast?

There is no need to change anything, just noticing what is going on.

Bringing your awareness to your mind.

Does your mind feel fast or slow?

Does your mind feel full of movement or slow and silent?

Noticing what is happening without judgement.

Bringing your awareness to your emotions. Just noticing how you feel here.

Do you feel sad or happy?

Do you feel angry or relaxed?

Do you feel fearful or full of peace?

Again, we are just noticing what we feel. There is no need to adjust anything.

Were any of your answers different from before?

In what way were they different?

Take a moment to be present with yourself, just enjoying any changes you have noticed.

This relaxation can be your natural state, but like anything in life practice is needed to grow skills. Consider relaxation like a skill to be learned. Daily practice will allow your natural state to be one of relaxation through time and repetition.

We're going to very gently come out of this experience. You can stay connected to this light flowing through your body into Earth throughout the day. However, by coming back into your body it makes sure you are grounded and not too "airy" feeling which can be disorientating.

Bringing your awareness to your sensation of touch.

What do you feel touching your body? Clothes? The floor beneath you? A chair you are sitting on?

What is the temperature of where you are?

Can you feel the sensation of gravity?

Coming into your sense of smell. What do you smell around you? It could be nothing, so just note that. It could be a light scent.

Coming into your sense of taste, just noticing how your mouth feels. Are there any flavours on your tongue? Perhaps running your tongue against your teeth and just feeling the sensation of your mouth as well.

Coming into your sense of hearing. Noticing any sounds around you. Noticing any light electronic sounds like air conditioning, heating, cars in the background, planes, or anything else that comes up. If you're in nature, perhaps the wind in the trees, or people in the background.

And finally, coming into your sense of sight. Very gently opening your eyes if they were closed, and taking in your surroundings. Noticing the colours, the light, the shadows, the textures, the shapes of objects, whatever draws your attention. Taking it all in without judgement.

And taking one final deep breath in, and out, as you come back into your body.

Taking a nice deep stretch if you need to.

Thank you for participating in this meditation. It is suggested to drink extra water and to keep your breathing steady throughout the day. You can re-listen to this meditation anytime you need for some extra energy in your life.

Have an energetic day!

Clear Your Mind | 60 Minutes | 1670 words

Hello and welcome to this guided meditation to help you clear your mind. In our modern world there seems to be an endless amount of distractions, emails, errands, and small tasks to do. With our smartphones always on us, people can reach us at any time with more responsibilities piling up. Here we will take sixty minutes to let go of all of these tasks to focus on relaxation.

Take a moment to make sure you won't be disturbed for the duration of this meditation.

Either sit or lie down in a comfortable position where you won't need to move around too much for the next sixty minutes. Make sure your spine is straight, and you feel relaxed.

Let go of your day.

Let go of any stress you may be carrying.

Let go of any worries you might have at the back of your mind.

Let go of any responsibilities you have.

Let go of what you do not need to focus on right now.

Taking some time to deepen your breath.

Slow, luxurious, calming breaths in and out.

Letting there be a small pause in between your inhalations and exhalations.

Perhaps letting your exhalations be a little longer than your inhalations.

Seeing if you can allow your belly to breathe, and not just your chest.

There is no right or wrong way to breathe, it's just about finding a rhythm that works best for your body. These are just suggestions.

See if you can enjoy the sensation of breathing.

Enjoying the sensation of cool air entering your body. Feeling it enter your nostrils, all the way down your throat, into your belly.

Feeling the warm air leave your belly, up your throat, and out of your nose.

Letting your breath slowly relax your body.

On each exhalation, letting a little bit of tension, heaviness, or stress evaporate from your body.

Letting go of anything you do not need, as if there was a gentle breeze carrying it away on your exhalations.

Feeling as if each inhalation allows relaxing, cooling energy to enter your body.

Each exhalation allows heaviness or stress to leave your body.

Breathing at a tempo that feels perfect for your individual body.

Starting with your feet and ankles, imagine you could breathe into your feet. Letting your breath fill your feet, and then on the exhalation taking away any tension, stress, or pain from the area.

Moving to your lower legs, breathing into here. Letting all tension, stress, or heaviness leave this area on the exhalations.

Moving into your knees, breathing into here, letting go of anything you no longer need.

Moving up to your upper legs, breathing into here, and releasing anything you no longer need on your exhalations.

Moving up to your hips, your groin, and your buttocks, breathing into here, and releasing anything you no longer need on your exhalations.

Moving up to your lower abdomen, and lower back. Breathing into here, and releasing anything no longer needed on your exhalations.

Moving up to your lower rib cage area, the middle of your torso, the middle of your back. Breathing into here, and releasing any stress, tension, or pain on the exhalation.

Moving up to your chest and upper back, breathing into here. Letting go of any tension or heaviness on the exhalations.

Moving up into your shoulders, breathing into the entire area, and releasing anything you no longer need on the exhalations.

Breathing into your upper arms, and releasing any tension, pain, or stress on the exhalations.

Breathing into your elbows, and releasing any tension here on the exhalations.

Breathing into your lower arms, and releasing any tension or unpleasant sensations on the exhalations.

Breathing into your wrists and hands, and releasing any tension, pain, or stress from this area on the exhalations.

Moving back up to your neck, breathing in here, and releasing all the stress and tension on the exhalations.

Moving up to your jaw, your lips, your mouth, and your lower cheeks. Breathing into here, and releasing tension on the exhalations.

Moving up to your upper cheeks, your eyes, and around to the back of your head. Breathing into this whole area, and releasing anything no longer needed on the exhalations.

Moving up to your forehead and the top of your head and skull, breathing into here, and letting go of any stress and tension on the exhalations.

Now, as if each breath filled your entire body, and each exhalation released air from your entire body, breathe as if you could feel it through every part of your body.

Letting the inhalations fill everything from the top of your head to the bottom of your feet.

Letting your exhalations release everything from the top of your head to the bottom of your feet.

I will go silent as you experience this.

Now we are going to calm down emotions that may feel turbulent sometimes. If at any point you feel too uncomfortable, simply bring your awareness to your breath again. Only experience what you feel comfortable trying.

As if you could feel the stress in your body- perhaps from your job, your responsibilities, your family life, your relationships, or whatever it is- where would the stress in your body be?

Is there any tension anywhere in your body?

If you cannot find a specific location of where stress is concentrated, just imagine this exercise using your entire body.

For those of you who have found a specific location in your body of tension or stress, breathe into the area.

Almost as if each breath gives this area love.

For some of you, it might feel really tight and uncomfortable to breathe here. It's kind of like we're massaging this part of your body using your breath. Let whatever sensations that come up, just come up, and release them using your exhalations.

Breathing into the area of tension, and releasing all of the tension with your exhalations.

Letting your breath be at a tempo that feels good for you.

I'm going to go quiet for a bit as you continue breathing into this area.

Just noticing any differences already in your body.

Let's move to a different location. Same thing as before. Is there another part of your body that feels stressed, perhaps tired, or in pain? Breathing into this area with loving breaths for a while.

If you cannot find another area that is full of tension, just breathing into your entire body.

Remembering that each inhalation fills this area with light cleansing air, and each exhalation takes any stress, tension, or pain away.

Letting yourself enjoy the sensation of breathing.

Knowing that by doing this experience, you may feel much lighter after.

I'm going to go quiet for a bit as you continue breathing.

Now imagine that your mind feels like a physical sensation. Each one of your thoughts has its own physical feeling to it. Positive thoughts feel light and airy. Stressful thoughts feel a bit more dense and heavy. It may feel a little funny, but just imagine that you could breathe into your brain. Imagine that you can breathe into your mind, and your thoughts.

Each inhalation brings your breath into your own mind, and fills it with cleansing, light energy.

Each exhalation releases any heavy, troubling, or stressful thoughts with it.

If you are a visual person, you can imagine that these thoughts float away like balloons in the wind.

If you prefer to just feel what is happening, imagine that any heaviness in your mind just drifts away like a cloud.

So breathing into your brain area, and exhaling out any heaviness.

Letting the inhalations fill your mind with light and love, and the exhalations releasing any tension or stress.

I'm going to go quiet for a bit as you continue breathing into your mind.

We're going to breathe into one last area today, which is your heart. Imagine breathing into your heart, and exhaling out any tension.

Even though the heart is a physical organ that keeps our bodies alive and happy, it also is a huge location for emotions and mental well-being. By breathing into this area alone, you are not only helping out your body physically, but you are also soothing down the emotions into a more peaceful state. The more you practice this, the more effective it is.

Breathing into your heart area. Enjoy that deep cooling breath filling up the entire area, and then exhaling out any tension, or emotions that come up.

Just imagine that any tension is released like balloons on the wind, or like gentle clouds drifting away. Whatever works best for you. There is no right or wrong way to experience this.

Just continue breathing into the heart area, and breathing out any tension or stress.

I'm going to go quiet one last time, as you breathe into your heart.

Now we're going to come back into your everyday life. Just remember that the more you practice meditation, the easier it will be for your natural state to feel calm and relaxed. Meditation is like a skill that needs to be practiced daily to feel its full effects in your everyday life.

Let's just come back into the sensations of your physical body.

Feeling the weight of gravity.

Feeling the sensation of fabric on your skin.

Feeling the temperature on your skin.

Smelling any scents in the room where you are, or your surroundings.

Tasting the flavors on your tongue.

Hearing any surrounding sounds. It could be low electronic humming, it could be nature, or it could be people in the background. Just noting it all.

Gently open your eyes and taking in the environment. Noticing any colours, textures, light versus shadow, and shapes.

Congratulations for completing this meditation today. It is recommended to keep your breathing slow and rhythmic throughout the rest of the day. Just go slowly and know that sometimes accomplishing something slowly but with awareness gets the job done better.

Thank you for listening, and have a tranquil day.

Visualize Your Ideal Day | 15 Minutes | 942 Words

Hello and welcome to this meditation for visualizing your ideal day. Here we will be using visualization, imagination, and manifestation to pull together your ideal reality. You can use this meditation every day, or just when you feel like you want to have more clarity in where you are going.

Our daily lives define our long-term future. Our long-term results are based on our daily habits. Habits can be quite challenging to change. However, if you know why you want to change your habits, it will be easier to modify your behavior, which will allow you to accomplish your goals. One of the ways to do this is to use visualization as a tool to trick your mind, body, and emotions into believing it's happening right now. This alters the way you think into a version of yourself where you have already achieved your goals. This will then change your daily habits through time, as you will function as someone who has already gotten there, versus someone who is trying to get there. As time passes, and with persistence, you can get to where you want to go in life. It comes down to the simple concept of repeating this vision every day mixed with modifying your behavior to get you a little bit closer to your destination.

To begin, I recommend you perform this meditation sitting up with your spine straight. You want to remain as present, alert, and energized as possible during this meditation. It may be beneficial to sit cross-legged on the ground so it is easier to remain grounded. If you cannot do that, sitting on a chair is perfectly okay as well. Listen to your body first.

Visualization is a tool to help us build clarity on what we want and what we don't want. Many times we are just unaware of what we want because we have never thought about it.

Before we begin, ask yourself what you want to see today:

Do you want to see your ideal day in your future ten years from now?
Do you want to see your ideal day today?
Do you want to see your ideal day when you get that new job, career, friend group, or house?

Do you want to see your ideal day when you find your soulmate, or when you will get married, or have that dream vacation?

Whatever it is, find one ideal day that you can focus your attention on during this meditation. You can choose this day to be about anything, there are no limits. Just pick something that excites you.

Take your time. Breathe as you ponder this.

Whatever you picked, just stick with it, have fun during this meditation. You will be guided through the entire experience.

Begin to focus on your breath.

As you breathe in imagine that you are pulling up energy from the ground into your body, and as you exhale you release energy back into the ground.

Breathe in, and pull up energy from the ground into your body.

Breathe out, releasing everything back into the ground.

Keep breathing in this way, as I suggest some things to release before we begin the visualization.

Releasing any fear, tension, or pain in the body or emotions.

Releasing any thoughts that are not helpful to you in life right now.

Releasing any confusion, anxiety, stress, or pain anywhere in your awareness.

Breathing in, and out. Feeling energy pulled up from the ground into your body, and exhaling out into the ground again.

Almost as if each inhalation brings in calming energy, and each exhalation releases anything you no longer need into the ground.

Allowing your breathing to be from the bottom of your abdomen.

Allowing your exhalations to extend further.

Allowing a pause to form between your breaths.

Breathing at a pace that is comfortable for you.

Inhaling up from the ground into your body.

Exhaling into the ground releasing anything you no longer need.

Imagine that your perfect, ideal day is happening around you right now.

Where are you?

Who are you with?

What are you wearing?

How are you standing?

What did you just eat, or have you not eaten yet?

How healthy do you feel?

How light do you feel?

What do you think of the word abundance now?

Have you accomplished more things in life?

Fill in any ideas, images, or concepts around you as you sit in this moment of time. Your ideal day.

What did you do when you woke up?

Did you travel anywhere, and how did you get there?

What did you accomplish today, or did you do nothing today and peacefully rest?

Let your imagination fill in any details that you wish. Let it roam free, and breathe through this.

Coming back into your body now, just noticing the sensation of your feet and your legs.

Notice the sensation of your torso.

Notice the sensation of your arms and your hands.

Notice the sensation of your neck and your head.

Notice how your body feels.

Just being present with what is going on.

How do you feel now?

Opening your eyes whenever you are ready.

Taking your time.

As simple as those questions were, they stimulate the imagination into considering what's possible. Before there may have been a hidden thought saying "I don't deserve that", but in an experience like this, it builds an awareness that you already have it. It may not be here physically yet, but you already have it mentally, emotionally and spiritually. It's very powerful, very simple, and works best when done every day.

Thank you for listening to this meditation. See you next time.

Manifesting Your Dreams | 60 Minutes | 2245 Words

Welcome to this guided meditation for manifesting your dreams! Manifestation is kind of like tapping into a world or reality where you already have what you desire. From this state, your actions are decided from a reality of someone who already has it and therefore deserves what they are seeking. It is a lot about what emotional state you are in. Even if you do not have what you desire yet, by feeling as though you have it now it opens up new doors of opportunities you may have otherwise missed. Perhaps there is a promotion just waiting to happen but if you do not see your potential you do not see the opportunity before you. The more you practice manifestation and understand its mechanics the easier it is to do! It is also helpful to know that manifestation does not always happen immediately. The reality is, some manifestations are so large it could take years for them to happen, but smaller ones could happen quickly. Patience will also be discussed later on and how it is tied into all of this.

Let us begin. Take a moment to get comfortable. Whether you are sitting or lying down, make sure your spine is straight and that you can remain here comfortably for the next sixty minutes. You may want to turn your electronics on to do not disturb if you have not already done so.

Bring your awareness to your breath, and relax.

Let go of anything you do not need to focus on right now. Bring your awareness to the present moment. Here and now, and nothing else.

Allow your life to feel simple. It is just about this one moment, right here.

Let breath move down your body into your abdomen. Breathing through your abdomen in a deep and slow fashion that is comfortable for you. Perhaps making your exhalations longer than your inhalations.

Feeling your body grounded into the Earth. Feeling gravity. Feeling a gentle heaviness of your body. That relaxing pull into the Earth.

Slowing everything down, your thoughts, your feelings, your sensations, into this moment.

Releasing what you do not need. Any thoughts that pop up, just letting them go. Any emotions that come up, letting them go. Any sensations that come up, letting them go.

Releasing any judgements you have of yourself, there is no right or wrong way to meditate, only being present with where you are.

Letting your feet relax. Feeling any tension or vibrating energy melt into the Earth. Perhaps imagining that you could breathe into your feet if that helps you connect.

Letting your lower legs and your knees relax. Breathing into here. Letting all the tension melt out of your legs into the Earth beneath you. Replacing it with a gentle, heavy relaxation.

Letting your upper legs relax. Breathing into here. Letting all the tension, anxiety, or stress melt away from here into the Earth beneath you. Feeling a gentle heaviness replacing that old energy. Enjoying the new sensations.

Letting your groin and your pelvic floor relax. Simply breathe into the area. Letting all tension and old sensations go into the floor, into the

Earth. Warm, gentle, and kind energy filling in its place.

Letting all the muscles in around your buttocks relax, just breathing into here, letting anything go. Releasing all judgement of allowing yourself to relax. Feeling a gentle relaxation replace the old energy.

Now to your hip area, relaxing all areas here. Where your legs join your torso, all the little tiny muscles. Breathing into here, and relaxing deeply. Letting all the strain, tension, and anxiety melt into the Earth.

Moving up to your lower belly, breathing into here. Letting everything go into the Earth beneath you. Letting gentle, kind energy replace the old energy.

Wrapping around to your hips and lower back, breathing into here, and letting it all go. Letting it melt into the Earth. Letting all the old and heavy sensations go, and replacing it with gentle warm energy.

Moving up into the middle of your back and waist, breathing into here. Letting all the tension or perhaps pain melt into the Earth beneath you.

Enjoy this experience as you feel a kinder, warmer energy replace the old energy in this area.

Wrapping around to the middle of your abdomen and all the organs inside, breathing into here. Letting it all go. Letting it all melt into the Earth. Replacing it with warm, kind, gentle energy.

Moving up into the lower rib cage area, just breathing into here. Letting all the tension go. Letting all the old emotions or sensations go. Replacing it with a gentle and soothing energy in its place.

Wrapping around the ribcage and including the same section on your back. Breathing into here. Letting all tension go. Feeling it melt into the Earth. Having gentle and soothing energy fill up this area instead.

Moving to your upper back, breathing into here, letting all the tension, stress, and anxiety go. Breathing in warming energy. Feeling old energy melt into the Earth as warm nurturing energy fills its place.

Wrapping around to the side of your ribcage and your chest area. Breathing into here. Letting everything go as it melts into the Earth away from your body forever. Feeling a warm nurturing energy filling up this area in its place.

Moving up to your shoulders and shoulder blades, including your armpits. Breathing into here. Letting everything go. All the tension, anxiety, stress built up here. Feeling the old energy melt into Earth, and in its place with each breath is warm, nurturing energy.

Moving to the upper arms and elbows, breathing into here. Letting everything go. Having the old energy melt into the Earth, and in its place is warm, soothing energy.

Moving to the lower arms, breathing into here. Letting everything go. Feeling any tension melt into the Earth. Having warm, soothing energy replace the old energy in this area.

Now the wrists and your hands, breathing into this area as all the tension and anxiety is melting into the Earth. Breathing into this area with warm nurturing energy in its place.

Moving back up to the clavicle bone area and your neck, breathing into this whole section, and feeling all the tension and stress melting into the ground, into the Earth. Letting it all go. Breathing in warm, nurturing energy in its place.

Breathing into your face and your head now, letting all the old tense energy go. Perhaps imagining that all of the stressful thoughts are leaving your brain as well, just melting off of your body into the Earth. As you breathe into here calm, warm energy enters the area instead.

And for a moment just enjoying how your body feels. Breathing gently and slowly at a pace comfortable with you. Letting any remaining old energy melt away from your body, and naturally be replaced with warm, soothing energy.

If your eyes are not already closed, I recommend closing them now. Using your imagination, answer these questions. Make it as colorful and fun as possible. There is no right or wrong answer, and you never have to share your answers with anyone if you do not wish to. This is for you alone, and no one else.

What is one thing that brings you joy in life? It could be something small like brushing your teeth, or large like planning out vacations with your loved ones. Think of anything that comes up.

How does this make you feel?

Where do you feel this good emotion in your body?

What does it make you want to do? Smile? Dance? Laugh? Sing? Whatever it is, just go with the most natural answer that comes up.

This state that you are in right now is what most questions coming up should be answered like. Feel the answers that you give in your physical body. It's not just about imagining it, it's about feeling it.

What is something that you want from life? It could be something big or small, but it is what we will be focusing on for the next little while, so make sure it can be explored. You can change it halfway through if you wish. Really feel the answer in your body. Bring as many sensations as you can into this experience.

This vision, goal, or idea you have, why do you think you want it? What can it give you?

Does anyone else in your life have this? How does that make you feel?

Can you remember from what age you wanted this?

Can you remember what caused you to want this, or has it always been a desire of yours?

If you had this, how would it make you feel?

Let's explore that in more detail. Imagine that you had it now.

Where are you?

What are you doing?

What do you see physically?

What do you hear?

What do you smell?

What do you taste?

What are you touching? With your body, or your hands?

How do you feel?

How relaxed are you, or joyful are you?

How old are you?

How far into the future is this?

Who is in your life?

Who is not in your life?

How are you dressed?

How do you stand?

How do you act?

What is different about you?

How do you think? Is it a calm mind, is it an active mind?

From this part of your life, imagine you could zoom out a bit and look at the day you had. What time did you wake up at?

What was your morning like?

What did you eat, or did you not eat?

How healthy are you?

What did you do around your mid-day?

What did you do in your afternoon?

What did you do in your evening?

What did you do at night?

How was your sleep?

How do you like this life of yours?

How does it make you feel?

Do you like this version of you?

What do you think you need to do to get here?

What do you think is fundamentally different from you and this future version of you?

See if this future version of you can see you and can talk to you.

If this future you could look at you and tell you something what would it be?

If you could ask this version of you anything, what would it be?

What is their response?

Does this person have a gift for you or a secret message to share?

Do you receive this?

Take a moment to thank this future you for sharing their life. This could be you one day, looking back at the version you are now.

Let's take a moment to just release this experience. The answers you gave are not going anywhere, they are in your heart. Feel free to just let all the answers, memories, or experiences go. They are with you still.

Breathing in, and letting everything go on the exhalation.

Breathing in, and letting it all go on the exhalation.

Giving a moment to thank yourself for experiencing this.

Coming back into the sensations of your body.

Coming back into the sensations of your breathing.

Wiggling your toes when you feel ready to, bringing sensation back to your feet.

Wiggling your fingers in your hands, bringing sensations here.

Taking little stretches when you feel ready.

Coming back into the present moment.

Perhaps opening your eyes and taking in the room.

Noticing the scents around you.

Noticing any sounds.

Noticing how your mouth tastes.

Noticing how your body feels.

Noticing the difference between how you felt now vs. how you felt before.

This meditation can be listened to as many times as you need. The more you practice manifestation, the more you will understand how it works. As with all things, most manifestations can take time to happen. It's kind of like you are building a blueprint or a target to work towards, and you have to do the actions so that all areas of your life can start to look like that reality. If you ever get frustrated that your life does not look like where you want to be, simply take a listen to this again, and remember that all we really want is to feel like we are in that life when we are getting frustrated. We are more guided by our feelings than by what is physically around us.

If we want a new job, we are mainly focusing on how that new job would make us feel. If we want a new house, we are mainly focusing on how that new home would make us feel. So you can feel that way anytime, just by imagining you have it now. That takes out a lot of the effort! This way it is as if your mind, emotions, and spirit already have it, and the rest is just patience as you take the actions needed to get to your physical reality.

Patience is something that is formed over time. It is okay to get frustrated, it is okay to want something, but it doesn't necessarily mean you can speed up the process. Some things just take a while. Whenever you want something to happen now, just put your hand over your heart and give your heart love. Your heart's needs will be met, just over some time.

Thank you for listening to this guided meditation. Have a wonderful rest of your day.

Self-Love and Compassion | 30 Minutes | 1133 Words

Hello and welcome. This meditation is dedicated to growing self love and compassion for yourself. Self love and compassion is based on seeing ourselves in a kind and understanding way. We all make mistakes, we all try our best, and we all want to be the best version of ourselves in some way. Everyone needs love. Love is a fuel for our lives. Love provides us with joy, happiness, peace, and prosperity. Without it, we would fall into depression, fatigue, illness, and heaviness. Love is indescribable, but in this meditation we will attempt to show you some fundamental ways to love yourself. It is easy and fun, however sometimes it is natural for emotions to come up. If at any point it becomes too uncomfortable, feel free to stop the recording. You can simply come back to this recording when you feel ready to. There is no rush.

Make sure you are sitting in a comfortable position for the next thirty minutes. It is recommended to sit up with your spine straight. You may want to turn your electronics on to do not disturb so you will not be interrupted during this time.

Become aware of how your body feels today. Sometimes it is easier to do this when you bring your awareness to your breath. All you have to do is notice what you feel physically today. As you breathe in and out, do you notice anywhere that feels stiff, tense, or sore? Take a moment to simply breathe, and be present with how your body feels.

We are bringing the awareness to anywhere in the body that feels stiff, tense or sore. If there are a few spots, pick the spot that feels the most noticeable. If there is nothing that feels tense, simply pick a place in your body that feels the least flexible and loose.

Wherever this place is on your body, bring your hands there and breathe into it. If you cannot reach it, just imagine that your hands are there and breathe into this area.

Slow your breathing down. Bring your attention into this area. Imagine that your lungs were in this area and you could breathe into it.

Each breath provides love and attention to the area.

Imagine that your hands are sending this area warmth, light, love, compassion, and whatever else it needs.

Your hands are there for this area.

This area is deeply loved and held right now.

Everything is okay.

Imagine warmth, light, love, and compassion being sent to this area. Sending it light it may not have received before.

All the tension and stress from this part of your body is just melting away with each breath.

Keep your breathing going at a slow and steady pace. It may be beneficial to breathe from the bottom of your belly. It may be beneficial to breathe from the back of your throat. Whatever feels best for you.

When you feel this area has received enough love, move to another place in the body. You may have to take a moment to breathe in silence and see which place feels tense. You may know immediately where the next place is. If you cannot reach it, imagine your hands are there.

Breathing into this area. Letting your hands send this area light and love. Feeling this area fill up with warmth. Feeling this area relax with each breath.

Being present with your breathing as you are with this part of your body.

Knowing that you are worthy of a relaxed and healthy body.

Imagining that all the tension and stress from this part of your body is just melting away with each breath.

Each breath in brings this area more light. Breathing into this area as if your lungs were here. Each exhalation releases any tension or stress.

Moving into another area of your body. If there is nowhere else, you can repeat an area if you wish.

Placing your hands over the area and breathing into here.

Sending this area warmth, love, and light with your hands.

Every breath brings in more warmth, every breath out releases any tension.

Moving into one more area of the body. Breathing into here, and letting everything go. Placing your hands over the area, and sending it warmth, love, light, and compassion.

Now, placing your hand over your heart, and breathing into your heart. Sending your heart love, light, and compassion.

Each inhalation brings in more love and compassion.

Each exhalation releases anything you wish to release, no matter how small or large.

Placing your hand over your lower abdomen or your sacral chakra area. Breathing into here. Sending this creative part of yourself love, warmth, and compassion.

Every inhalation brings in more love and compassion.

Every exhalation releases anything you wish to release.

Placing your hand over your upper abdomen, where it is the bottom of your ribcage. Breathing into this area.

Every inhalation brings in more love and compassion.

Every exhalation releases anything you wish to release.

Letting your hands go and resting them on your legs. Breathe into your whole body, as if your whole body were your lungs.

Bringing in light, love, and compassion to every cell in your body.

And on your exhalations, releasing anything you no longer need.

Repeating these words either in your mind or out loud. See if you can feel the truth of these words in your body. Don't just repeat them without anything behind it. Feel the emotional connection to these words. You can place your hand over your heart if it helps to connect.

I love all that I am.

I love who I am.

I am compassionate to all parts of myself.

I am understanding to all parts of myself.

I am my own mother.

I am my own father.

I am my own source of energy.

I love my mind.

I love my body.

I love my emotions.

I love my energy.

I love my life.

I love how I move through life.

I appreciate everything I have done in this life.

I appreciate that I am taking the time to listen to a self-love meditation.

I appreciate that I look after myself.

I appreciate who I am.

I appreciate what I have done.

I appreciate where I am going.

I appreciate all that I am, in all ways.

My love for myself is endless.

I have an abundance of love in my life.

I am worthy of all that I ask for.

I am worthy of a life full of love and compassion.

Ending the affirmations, taking a moment to feel those words in your body.

Thank you for listening to this meditation. Move through your day slowly today. Make sure you have compassion and self care for yourself first. Have a love-filled day.

Meet Your Inner Child | 60 Minutes | 2326 Words

Hello and welcome to this guided meditation for inner child healing. As lovely as it is to work with our inner child, sometimes it can be emotional. If you get too overwhelmed in this meditation, feel free to turn off this recording and listen to it at a later date. There is no rush.

Our inner children are the homes to our creativity, playfulness, sense of adventure, sense of wonder, humility, and so much more. Our society tends to put an emphasis on our inner adults: confidence, assuredness, ability to accomplish tasks, sense of power, etcetera. However, the inner child works through vulnerability. It does not come out to play unless it feels safe to do so. It's kind of like a bunny in a meadow. If the bunny feels that there is someone there that will not want to respect it and play with it, it probably will not come out of it's home. The inner child is the same way, it will not reveal itself to you unless it feels safe to do so. In this meditation, we will create a safe environment so that you can meet your inner child and begin forming a connection with them.

Let's first calm down your body.

Let go of your day. Let go of any stress. Let go of any anxiety. Let go of any worries.

Breathing in soothing energy, and releasing anything you wish to release on your exhalations.

Breathing from the bottom of your torso.

Letting your breaths be slow and languid.

Feeling them flow in and out of your body at a peaceful tempo.

Feeling the top of your head relax.

Feeling your forehead relax.

Feeling your scalp relax.

Feeling your eyes relax.

Feeling your cheeks relax.

Feeling your mouth relax.

Feeling your tongue relax.

Feeling your jaw relax.

Feeling your neck relax.

Feeling your collar bone area at the top of your torso relax.

Feeling your shoulders and armpit area relax.

Feeling your upper arms relax.

Feeling your elbows relax.

Feeling your wrists relax.

Feeling your hands relax, and all of your fingers.

Feeling your chest relax.

Feeling your shoulder blades relax.

Feeling your upper back relax.

Feeling your spine relax.

Feeling your mid-back relax.

Feeling your abdomen relax.

Feeling your lower back relax.

Feeling your lower abdomen relax.

Feeling your hips relax.

Feeling your groin and pelvic floor relax.

Feeling your buttocks relax.

Feeling your upper legs relax.

Feeling your knees relax.

Feeling your lower legs relax.

Feeling your ankles relax.

Feeling your feet relax.

Letting your entire body be with the sensation of relaxation.

Breathing in, and releasing anything you wish to let go of on the exhalations.

Breathing in, and letting everything go on your exhalations.

Breathing in, and letting everything go on your exhalations.

Close your eyes if you have not already done so.

Just follow along with what I am saying and let your imagination fill in the rest.

Imagine that you are in a clearing in a private forest. It's a meadow, filled with beautiful plants, rich scents, and lush greenery all around you. A dense forest surrounds the meadow and you instinctively know you are safe here.

In this meadow there is a small house that could fit a child, and nothing more. Running beside the house is a small stream, giving the environment the tranquil sound of a light stream flowing away from your direction.

It smells of a healthy forest. You hear the sounds of birds, insects, the stream, and the trees swaying in the wind.

You see a bright blue sky and lush green landscape all around you.

You breathe in the fresh air, and breathe out.

This place makes you feel comfortable, it's hard to tell why. You are just safe here.

You are bare feet on the grass, and you feel it's soft floor on the soles of your feet.

The little house is ahead of you. You know that your inner child lives here. There's a tiny chimney with smoke coming out of it. Someone is home.

You walk up to the house, kneel down, and knock on the door.

Someone opens it, and it is you, from when you were a child.

How are they dressed?

How do they look?

How do they greet you?

Your inner child may have a lot to tell you, or they may be quiet.

Just be present with your child. Have no intentions, let them lead this moment. Just witness who they are.

Keep your breathing going as you be with your child. Perhaps they are talking, perhaps you are both in silence.

Invite them over to the stream. This stream is special. Anyone who goes into it is immediately healed from any fear, pain, sorrow, and sadness.

Does your child have any pain they need to release? Any sadness in their heart?

If not, does your child want to play in the stream?

If your child does not want to play in the stream, just follow along with what they want to do and let this be background noise for a moment.

Bringing your child to the stream, perhaps hand in hand, perhaps they are following you. You get into the water first.

Your clothing gets wet, but it's a pleasant temperature. It smells like fresh spring water.

You sit down in the current, and you feel the current already taking away any stress, pain, suffering, or sorrow from your own body.

You invite your child to join you.

When they are in the water, make sure the water touches all parts of their skin. Pour it on their hair gently. Wash their face with it. Be gentle with them, they're just a child.

Witness as this magical stream takes away the pain from the child's eyes. Witness as the child looks brighter with every passing moment. Keep your breathing steady as you are here.

Perhaps just take some time with your child to play in the water.

Perhaps take some time to both rest in the water.

Do whatever you wish with your inner child. You are safe here.

For anyone who did not want to play in the water, you can join this part now. In this meadow, both of you can magically produce anything you wish. You can instantaneously manifest a jungle gym, a theme park, a house, animals, friends, whatever you wish.

Is there anything that both of you would like to play with?

Make it as big or as special as you want.

The meadow can magically grow in size.

Whatever you manifested, go towards it together. As you step out of the water your clothes can change into something dry, or even a new outfit. Have fun, and let your imagination choose what you do here.

Together, go towards what you just manifested. Perhaps hand in hand, perhaps you leading the way, whatever feels best for both of you.

Play, dance, sing, witness, or do whatever feels best with what you just manifested together. Have fun with it!

As your imagination is so creative, I will simply guide you through handling your emotions for now.

Breathe through your abdomen as you experience this.

Witness the joy, happiness, peace, or love in your child's eyes.

Feel the emotions coming up in you.

Breathe deep into your body.

Feel your connection growing with your child in every passing moment.

Know that any time you want to experience this, you can just come back into the meadow. There is no rush. You have your whole lives together!

Breathing in through your abdomen. Breathing out into peace.

When you are ready, you and your inner child may need to go home to eat. A lot has happened. It's healthy to take this slow and refuel your energy.

Since you are still in the meadow, go back to your child's home. It's still made for a child size, so it won't fit an adult. However, since in this meadow, whatever you wish comes true, you can change the house.

Would you like to change the house with your inner child into a size that could fit you?

With your child's permission, begin to grow the house.

Put it into a size that makes your child feel safe but that you can move around in.

Add as many details as you wish to the house. Perhaps you add a fence. Perhaps you add a garden. Perhaps you add some animals. Perhaps you add protection for the child's house with a totem. Whatever feels best for your heart.

When you are ready, go into the house with your child.

When you are not here, this is where your child will live. Make sure it is a healthy environment for a child. Do you want to add any furniture, any toys, any safety to the environment? Have you and your child change the inside of the home to fit what feels best for both of you.

Breathing as you do this.

Now, together, make a wonderful healthy meal with your child. Teach the child how to cook, even if you don't know how to cook yourself. It's all imagination.

Pull together some healthy foods, and take your time preparing a meal together.

Breathing through your abdomen, letting your emotions flow through you.

Perhaps your inner kid has things they want to tell you as you cook together.

When your meal is finished, either eat it in the house, or outside.

As everything is set up, watch as your child takes a bite and their reaction to the food. Whether they like it or don't like it, it is wonderful to see that they feel safe to show you their true emotions.

Just spend some time eating together, and allowing the child to eat or not eat whatever they choose.

Breathing in this experience. Letting your imagination have fun.

Perhaps there are some things you want to share with your inner child.

Time is an illusion here, and the sun is showing it's the late afternoon. It's time to wind down for the day. Your child had so much fun, but it may be good for them to take a nap, and for you to go back to your life. You can come back here anytime.

Making sure your child has a safe and healthy bedroom to sleep in, bring them to bed and tuck them in. Give them what they need, perhaps a stuffed animal, perhaps some water, perhaps a hug.

Tell them how wonderful your time together was for you.

See if they have anything they want to share until the next time they see you.

Say goodbye for now, and leave their room, and then their home, and close the door.

As you look around this meadow, already so different from when you came in just a little while ago, know that this place is safe for your inner child.

Congratulate yourself for having spent the imaginary day with your inner child. You met, healed together, played together, ate together, and now they are safely sleeping. Everything is good here.

This place is alive in your heart, so to come back, you can just listen to this guided meditation again. Even though we used your imagination through this experience, your unconscious mind, body, and emotions cannot tell the difference between what is real and imaginary. It was real for your body.

Taking some time to step out of this meadow in a way that suits you. Perhaps closing it down and storing it in a book you keep in your heart. Perhaps stepping out of it like a dimensional gateway into your life again. Perhaps vanishing out of it like magic back into your body. Have fun with it.

As you are back into your body, pay attention to your feet. Notice how they feel.

Bring your awareness to your lower legs, just noticing how they feel.

Bring your awareness to your upper legs, just noticing how they feel.

Bring your awareness to your lower torso, just noticing how everything feels.

Bring your awareness to your upper torso, just noticing how everything feels.

Bring your awareness to your upper arms, just noticing how they feel.

Bring your awareness to your lower arms, just noticing how they feel.

Bring your awareness to your hands, just noticing how they feel.

Bring your awareness to your neck and head, just noticing how it all feels.

Breathing into your body, and exhaling out.

Coming into your sense of smell, noticing any surrounding smells.

Coming into your sense of hearing, noticing any surrounding sounds.

Coming into your sense of taste, noticing any flavors on your tongue.

Coming into your sense of touch, noticing how your body feels. How it is to have the fabric against your body.

Coming into your sense of sight. Opening your eyes when you are ready and gently taking in your surroundings.

Taking a gentle stretch with your body.

Coming back into the environment you are in.

This was an imagination exercise to help you meet your inner child. Your inner child is alive inside your body, however sometimes it is helpful to make it an external inner child so you can more easily meet them. Your imagination is very powerful in that it can take intangible concepts and make it easy for you to perceive. You actually had that experience with your inner child, but it just was through a playful imagination. You may notice a part of you feels happier or lighter, that's probably your inner child within your body. You may notice a part of you feels proud or content, that's probably your inner adult within your body who played with the child. We have complex systems inside of us, through these methods we get to meet ourselves in new ways. You can come back into this meditation anytime you wish to meet your inner child again.

Thank you for listening to this meditation and have a wonderful day.

www.ingramcontent.com/pod-product-compliance
Lightning Source LLC
Chambersburg PA
CBHW071814080526
44589CB00012B/788